Includes Answer Key

Adapted by Anne Prucha
Original content by Nuria López-Ortega

Supplementary Activities Book
for
MOSAICOS

Spanish as a World Language
Fifth Edition

Matilde Olivella de Castells (Late)
Emerita, California State University, Los Angeles

Elizabeth E. Guzmán
University of Iowa

Paloma Lapuerta
Central Connecticut State University

Judith E. Liskin-Gasparro
University of Iowa

Prentice Hall
Upper Saddle River London Singapore Toronto
Tokyo Sydney Hong Kong Mexico City

Executive Editor: Julia Caballero
Development Editors: Elizabeth Lantz, Celia Meana
Executive Marketing Manager: Kris Ellis-Levy
Senior Marketing Manager: Denise Miller
Marketing Coordinator: William J. Bliss
Senior Managing Editor: Mary Rottino
Associate Managing Editor: Janice Stangel
Project Manager: Manuel Echevarria
Development Editor for Assessment: Melissa Marolla Brown
Media Editor: Meriel Martínez
Senior Media Editor: Samantha Alducin
Art Manager: Gail Cocker
Assistant Editor/Editorial Coordinator: Jennifer Murphy
Manufacturing Buyer: Cathleen Petersen
Manager, Print Production: Brian Mackey
Editorial Assistant: Andrea Arias
Publisher: Phil Miller
Composition/Full-Service Project Management: Macmillan Publishing Solutions
Printer/Binder: OPM

This book was set in 12/14 Times New Roman.

10 9 8 7 6 5 4 3 2 1

Prentice Hall
is an imprint of

www.pearsonhighered.com

ISBN 10:   0-205-66432-6
ISBN 13: 978-0-205-66432-0

Contents

Introduction

To the student and the instructor:

The Supplementary Activities Book for *Mosaicos* offers in-class activities for each chapter of the fifth edition *Mosaicos* program. This manual is designed to give students and teachers additional in-class tasks and activities beyond those of the textbook and the student ancillaries.

The format of each chapter correlates closely to the sections of the textbook, with a series of activities related to each section of the chapter. Many of the activities presented in this manual contain two or three stages, or "pasos." These guide the students from checklists and information-gathering activities to structured writing and oral reports involving, in some cases, Internet research on specific topics of each chapter. Most of the activities require group or pair work, but many can be modified to better serve the learning needs of a specific group of students. While group or pair work is encouraged, teachers may assign the first phase or "paso" of an activity as individual homework and complete the rest of the activity in class. For instance, instructors may assign information-gathering sections as homework, and complete the rest of the activity during class time. Other activities can be modified for use in a multimedia classroom as on-line activities.

Finally, most chapters contain a crossword puzzle or a "sopa de letras" that correlates to the vocabulary studied in the chapter. Students are encouraged to review vocabulary and grammar sections to better complete these activities.

While some activities require a "correct" answer, many of them have open-ended answers based on the students' personal experience, creativity, or information-gathering skills. Thus, instructors are encouraged to carefully review each activity and brainstorm on model answers for open-ended activities before presenting them to students. An answer key at the end of the manual provides correct answers to those activities that require a specific response. In some cases, model answers have been given.

CAPÍTULO

PRELIMINAR

Bienvenidos

P-1 Las presentaciones. Paso 1. With a classmate, decide what level of formality is appropriate when being introduced to the following people. Decide whether you would use **tú**, **usted**, or **ustedes**. (Your opinions may differ in some of these situations.):

	TÚ	USTED	USTEDES
1. a member of your college baseball team			
2. the president of your college			
3. your neighbor's teenage son			
4. your fiancé(e)'s parents			
5. an older coworker			
6. a friend of a friend			
7. a young pop star			
8. your boss (younger than you)			
9. your classmates			
10. a child you babysit for			

Nombre: _____   **Fecha:** _____

Paso 2. Now, write two short dialogues in which you introduce yourself in two of the situations presented above. Use the expressions learned in *Las presentaciones* on page 4 i your textbook.

Situación #____

Tú: _____

____: _____

Tú: _____

____: _____

Situación #____

Tú: _____

____: _____

Tú: _____

____: _____

P-2 Los saludos y las despedidas. Decide whether the following expressions are greeting or farewell expressions:

	SALUDO	**DESPIDIDA**
1. hasta luego		
2. buenos días		
3. hola		
4. adiós		
5. buenas noches		
6. chao		

P-3 Expresiones de cortesía. Decide what would be the best apology or expression of courtesy in the following situations:

1. You hit somebody with your elbow in a crowded bus . . .

2. You need to make your way out in a crowded movie theater . . .

3. You are about to place your order at a café . . .

4. You hear that your friend's grandfather fell down the stairs and broke his arm . . .

5. A friend treats you to ice cream after class . . .

6. Your friend answers back . . .

a. gracias

b. de nada

c. lo siento

d. por favor

e. con permiso

f. perdón

P-4 El alfabeto. Think of five capitals of five Hispanic countries (use the maps at the front and the back of the book to help you a little in case you cannot come up with correct spelling). Write down the name of the countries on a piece of paper and give it to your classmate. Your classmate must guess the name of the capital and spell it correctly to you. The one who gets more capitals and spellings correct wins!

MODELO: Chile → Santiago de Chile
    E1: *¿Cuál es la capital de Chile?*
    E2: *Santiago de Chile*
    E1: *Muy bien. ¿Y cómo se escribe?*
    E2: *s-a-n-t-i-a-g-o-d-e-c-h-i-l-e*
    E1: *¡Excelente!*

	PAÍS	**CAPITAL**
1.	_____	_____
2.	_____	_____
3.	_____	_____
4.	_____	_____
5.	_____	_____

P-5 Identificación y descripción de personas. Paso 1. Describe yourself to a group of three classmates. Use adjectives already learned in the chapter.

MODELO: E1: *Me llamo Manuel. Soy inteligente y activo. No soy sentimental.*

Paso 2. Once everybody has described himself/herself, choose one classmate of the group present him or her to the whole classroom. Give as much detail as you can. Your other classmates will ask you who he or she is.

MODELO: E2/E3: *Es activo e inteligente, pero no es sentimental.*
  E4: *¿Es Miguel?*
  E2/E3: *¡No, es Manuel!*

P-6 Los cognados. Some words in Spanish and English look similar but mean very differ things. Match the following two lists of words by their meanings, not by their appearance!

Check your answers with your classmate and comment on the differences.

1. success   **a.** avergonzado/a

2. exit   **b.** carta

3. embarrassed   **c.** éxito

4. lecture   **d.** compasivo/a

5. letter   **e.** salida

6. large   **f.** tarjeta

7. sympathetic   **g.** conferencia

8. card   **h.** grande

P-7 ¿Qué hay en el salón de clase? There are eight hidden classroom objects in the following word puzzle. Can you find them?

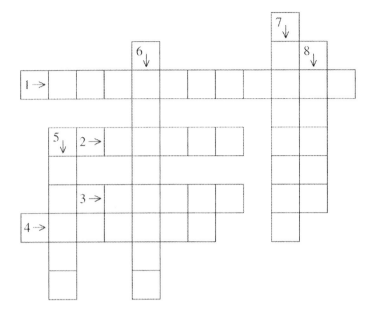

1. It is essential for your math problems.

2. Without it, you cannot write!

3. Old papers and waste go here.

4. You need them to study.

5. You sit on it.

6. You write your notes on it.

7. You pack and carry your books in it every morning.

8. It tells the time.

P-8 ¿Dónde está? ¿Dónde están los objetos y las personas? Ask a classmate where th[...] and people in the picture are located in relation to each other.

MODELO: E1: *¿Dónde está Marisa?*
             E2: *Marisa está enfrente de Javier.*

P-9 Los números de 0–99. Los números y la personalidad. Paso 1.

With a classmate, invent a list of adjectives you know in Spanish. Assign three adjectives t[...] each number from 1 to 9 (you can repeat adjectives occasionally):

1 = _____, _____, _____.

2 = _____, _____, _____.

3 = _____, _____, _____.

4 = _____, _____, _____.

5 = _____, _____, _____.

6 = _____, _____, _____.

7 = _____, _____, _____.

8 = _____, _____, _____.

9 = _____, _____, _____.

Nombre: _____   **Fecha:** _____ ■

Paso 2. Write down your classmate's full name (first, middle, last) in the first line of boxes. Then, assign a number to each letter, as listed below the box.

MODELO:

M	A	R	I	O		R	A	M	O	N		R	A	M	I	R	E	Z				
4	1	9	9	6		9	1	4	6	5		9	1	4	9	9	5	8				

1 →   A   J   S

2 →   B   K   T

3 →   C   L   U

4 →   D   M   V

5 →   E   N   W

6 →   F   O   X

7 →   G   P   Y

8 →   H   Q   Z

9 →   I   R

El nombre de tu compañero:

Capítulo preliminar Bienvenidos ■ 7

Paso 3. Add the numbers of each name, writing in letter the numbers in the following fas▐ (first add the corresponding numbers, to get a new two-digit number; then, add those two digits to get a final number):

Mario: <u>uno + tres + tres + nueve + seis</u> = <u>veintinueve</u> (29) → <u>dos + nueve</u> (2+9) = <u>once</u> (▐

Ramón: <u>nueve + uno + cuatro + seis + cinco</u> = 25 → <u>veinticinco</u> (25) → <u>dos + cinco</u> (2+5) = <u>siete</u> (7)

Ramírez: <u>nueve + uno + cuatro + nueve + nueve + cinco + ocho</u> = <u>cuarenta y cinco</u> (45) → <u>cuatro + cinco</u> (4+5) = <u>nueve</u> (9)

Do this with your classmate's name:

- _____ : _____ =

_____ → _____ = _____

- _____ : _____ =

_____ → _____ = _____

- _____ : _____ =

_____ → _____ = _____

- _____ : _____ =

_____ → _____ = _____

Paso 4. Now, add the final numbers from the names in the following fashion:

MODELO: once + siete + nueve = veintisiete (27) → dos + siete (2+7) = nueve (9)

Match the above number to the adjectives you assigned to each number, and describe your classmate to him or her and to the whole class!

MODELO: *Mario es el número nueve. Él es simpático, inteligente y muy sentimental.*

¿Cómo es tu compañero o compañera? ¿Es sentimental? ¿Es inteligente? ¿O es arrogante?...

P-10 Los meses del año y los días de la semana. With a calendar, check these important dates and days of the week for these events during this year and the next:

¿Cuándo es…?   ¿Qué día de la semana es…?

1. El Día de los Enamorados (*Valentine's Day*)

2. El Día de Acción de Gracias (*Thanksgiving Day*)

3. Tu cumpleaños

4. El cumpleaños de tu mamá

5. Las vacaciones de invierno (*winter break*)

6. El Día del Trabajo (*Labor Day*)

P-11 Las horas. You and your friend are going to the movies on Saturday.

Student A: You have the titles of the movies (see below) but do not have the show times, so you will ask your friend the times for each movie. Make sure you write down the times!

Student B: You got the show times and are calling your friend on the phone to decide which show to see (see the Appendix, page 221).

PELÍCULA	SESIONES			
La mujer araña				
La casa de los espíritus				
Diarios de motocicleta				
Hable con ella				
Troya				

P-12 Las expresiones útiles. Match the following expressions with their pictures:

1. vaya a la pizarra

2. abra el libro

3. pregúntele a su compañero

4. repita

5. siéntese

6. lea

a.   b.   c.

d.   e.   f.

P-13 Los meses del año y las tradiciones. Your friend came back from Spain singing these funny lyrics after she heard them in the streets of Pamplona during the celebration of *San Fermín* (the running of the bulls). You can help her. With some patience and your knowledge of the information from the *Capítulo preliminar*, fill in the blanks for the following lines of this traditional Spanish song.

Uno de enero,

(1)_____ de febrero,

tres de (2)_____,

(3)_____ de (4)_____.

cinco de mayo,

seis de (5)_____,

(6)_____ de Julio: ¡¡San Fermín!!

A Pamplona hemos de ir,	*To Pamplona we must go*
Con una bota, con una bota,	*with a wineskin*
A Pamplona hemos de ir,	*to Pamplona we must go*
Con una bota, y un calcetín	*with a wineskin and a sock*

(Note: This is a traditional Spanish song sung during *San Fermín*, the world-famous holiday during which the running of the bulls takes place, in Pamplona, Northern Spain.)

CAPÍTULO

1

En la universidad

A PRIMERA VISTA

1-1 Ensalada de letras. Do you know the meanings of the following nonsense words? Rearrange the letters of the following words to create vocabulary related to your school activities. Match your answers with the correct article (**el**, **la**, **los**, **las**) from the column on the right.

1. molachis   _____   **a.** el

2. artea   _____   **b.** las

3. facé   _____   **c.** la

4. palzas   _____   **d.** los

5. botolarioras   _____   **e.** la

6. duversinadi   _____   **f.** las

1-2 Sopa de letras. Paso 1. Find the adjectives from the list below in the following puzz

difícil	aburrido	bonitos	fácil
estudioso	bueno	grandes	favorita

B	R	E	V	I	U	A	F	S	H	O
L	O	A	S	E	D	N	A	R	G	K
A	S	O	L	T	X	H	V	E	L	J
Q	O	E	V	T	U	G	O	U	D	N
X	T	I	M	M	R	D	R	E	V	I
H	I	Ñ	K	D	I	F	I	C	I	L
Z	N	D	E	R	P	W	T	O	I	M
Y	O	S	R	M	Q	V	A	C	S	E
C	B	U	E	N	O	P	A	F	H	O
D	B	R	T	Z	G	F	V	U	B	Y
A	G	C	I	U	W	X	D	I	J	Ñ

Paso 2. Now write the words you found in the following blank spaces.

1. No es _____ estudiar toda la noche.

2. Los cuartos en la residencia de estudiantes son muy _____ y _____.

3. La antropología es _____ este semestre, pero la psicología es muy

_____.

4. No veo el noticiero porque es _____.

5. Mi compañero de cuarto es muy _____. Su asignatura _____ es la historia.

FUNCIONES Y FORMAS

1. Present tense of regular –ar verbs

1-3 Conversación de teléfono. Your classmate Carmen's mother wants to know everything about Carmen's friends and her activities at the Universidad de Salamanca. Complete Carmen and her mother's telephone conversation.

MAMÁ: Carmen, hija, ¿cómo se llama tu mejor amiga?

CARMEN: Mi mejor amiga (1) _____ Carmen, como yo. También tengo un buen
amigo, (2) _____ David.

MAMÁ: Ah, qué coincidencia, Carmen y Carmen... ¿Y qué clases toma Carmen?

CARMEN: (3) _____ biología, matemáticas y estadística. Yo sólo (*only*)
(4) _____ una clase con ella, la de estadística. David no
(5) _____ ninguna clase con nosotras.

MAMÁ: ¿Y dónde estudias todas las tardes?

CARMEN: Mamá, ¡yo no (6) _____ por las tardes, porque trabajo en la oficina!
(7) _____ en el apartamento, generalmente por las noches.

MAMÁ: ¡Uy, sí es verdad! Entonces, ¿cuándo hablas con los amigos? ¿y dónde?

CARMEN: Emm, no sé, a veces, los fines de semana, (8) _____ café con ellos en
el bar de la universidad. Otras veces, ellos (9) _____ TV en mi
apartamento por la noche.

MAMÁ: ¿Y cuánto cuesta la discoteca? ¿Es cara?

CARMEN: No, no (10) _____ cara, sólo (11) _____ cinco euros para
los estudiantes. Bueno mamá, tengo que dejarte, ¡mi clase de estadística es a las
8:30 y (12) _____ el autobús en cinco minutos!

MAMÁ: Bueno hija, hasta mañana entonces.

CARMEN: ¡Un beso! ¡Chao!

2. Present tense of regular –*er* and –*ir* verbs

1-4 Tu compañero/a y tú. Using the following list of verbs, tell about you and your frie
Who does what and when?

    comer   aprender   escribir

    vivir   leer

MODELO: Yo **como** en la cafetería, pero mi compañero siempre **come** en un restaurante c
              sus amigos.

1. Yo _____

      pero _____ (nombre) _____

2. Yo _____

      pero _____ (nombre) _____

3. Yo _____

      pero _____ (nombre) _____

4. Yo _____

      pero _____ (nombre) _____

5. Yo _____

      pero _____ (nombre) _____

3. Articles and nouns

1-5 Los materiales de trabajo. Paso 1. Carmen makes a list every night of the materials
she will need to pack for school.

Add the definite articles next to the nouns provided on her list.

(1) _____ *libro de historia*   *(4)* _____ *plumas de colores*

(2) _____ *cuadernos de estadística y biología*   *(5)* _____ *calculadora*

(3) _____ *lápices y*   *¡(6)* _____ *tarea de matemáticas!*

Paso 2. Now, help Carmen with a list of things to buy at the bookstore. Provide the indefinite articles next to the nouns.

(1) _____ diccionario científico

(2) _____ mochila para la computadora

*(3) _____ cuadernos para dibujo (*drawing*)*

(4) _____ tarjetas postales

¡(5) _____ mapa de la ciudad!

4. Present tense of *estar*

1-6   El plano de la universidad. Paso 1. Decide the gender of the following nouns. Write the correct definite article next to each word.
Places:

1. _____ biblioteca

2. _____ cafetería

3. _____ clínica

4. _____ Facultad de Humanidades

5. _____ gimnasio

6. _____ laboratorio de idiomas

7. _____ librería

8. _____ museo

9. _____ plaza

10. _____ teatro

El plano de la universidad

Student A

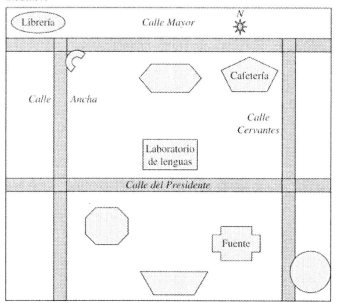

Paso 2

Student A: In your architecture class, your professor asks you to develop a modern de for a university campus. Your classmate started it, but he/she is sick and you need to finis the project over the phone with him/her. Together, you will complete the campus layout presented on this page with information you already know in Spanish.

Ask student B where the buildings and places are located in the map. You will also ne to discuss where to place additional buildings and places not decided yet in his/her layout.

Student B: In your architecture class, your professor asks you to develop a modern des for a university campus. You started a project for your architecture professor, but you are sick and need to give the information, over the phone, to a classmate who will present it to your professor tomorrow morning in class. Your classmate has the layout but does not hav the location of buildings. Together, you will complete the following campus layout with information you already know in Spanish.

You will answer your classmate's questions regarding the location and position of buildings and places. You will need to decide where you will put other buildings and place still not decided in your layout. Your campus map is located on the *Apéndice* of this manu; on page 222.

Get on the phone with your classmate and figure out the locations of these sites.

MODELO: E1: *Oye, ¿Dónde está la librería?*
   E2: *La librería está en la calle Mayor, al lado de la puerta de la Universidad.*
   E1: *Bien./Vale.*

When you have finished, present your campus maps to the teacher and the class. You can display them on the board or share them and explain them to other students in your class.

5. Interrogative words

1-7 David, el estudiante americano. Paso 1. Decide which question goes with each of the following statements by David, an American student at the Universidad de Salamanca:

a. Estudio matemáticas, sociología y estadística.

b. La universidad de Salamanca es muy antigua y bonita, de estilo gótico. Tiene más de cinco siglos.

c. No sé exactamente . . ., pero ¡hay muchos estudiantes en mis clases!

d. La biblioteca está cerca del patio central.

e. Mi aula es la de las ventanas grandes.

f. ¡Porque necesito estudiar para el examen de matemáticas!

g. ¡Uf! ¡Estoy súper contento!

1. ¿Cuál es tu aula?

2. ¿Qué asignaturas tomas este semestre?

3. ¿Cuántos estudiantes hay en cada (*each*) clase?

4. Hoy es domingo. ¿Por qué estás en el campus?

5. ¿Cómo es la arquitectura de la universidad?

6. ¿Cómo estás?

7. ¿Dónde está la biblioteca?

Paso 2. With a classmate: Now, create five more questions you would like to ask a student at the Universidad de Salamanca if you had the opportunity, using some of the question words in *Paso 1*.

1. _____

2. _____

3. _____

4. _____

5. _____

Paso 3. With your classmate present your questions and answers to the class. One of you will ask the questions and the other will play the role of David and answer the questions.

MOSAICOS

1-8 Encuesta sociológica a los estudiantes de la clase. Your sociology professor has as~
the class to do a survey on the social habits of college students on campus. You have a lis~
actions that, according to some studies, are common among college students.

Paso 1. Go around the class asking whether your classmates do the following things. The~
using an interrogative pronoun, ask them when, where, how, or why they do or don't do t~
things.

MODELO: E1: *¿Estudias inglés?*
E2: *No, no estudio inglés.*
E1: *¿Y por qué no?*
E2: *Porque el inglés es aburrido.*

ACCIONES: **¿QUIÉN?**   **CIRCUNSTANCI~**

estudiar inglés

hablar muchas lenguas

escuchar música en español

llegar a la universidad a las ocho de la mañana

sacar buenas notas

trabajar con computadoras mac

trabajar con computadoras pc

trabajar en una oficina

estudiar en la cafetería

escuchar las noticias en la radio

mirar las noticias en la televisión

estudiar por la noche

bailar los fines de semana en fiestas

mirar películas en el cine

comprar comida en el supermercado

(E1 writes down the name of the student on the appropriate column and the circumstance—
where, when, how, why—then moves on to next student.)

Paso 2. Now, inform your class about students' practices. Your teacher will ask you the following question, which you need to answer.

MODELO: PROFESORA: ¿Quién tiene información sobre Randall?
             E1:   *Randall no estudia inglés. El inglés es aburrido.*

1-9   Informe sociológico. Paso 1. Compare your answers to the previous activity with those of a classmate. Rank five to ten activities your classmates do from more common to less common, as well as the circumstances of those activities.

ACCIÓN:

1. _____

2. _____

3. _____

4. _____

5. _____

Paso 2. With your classmate, you are going to write a report for your sociology professor about the typical college student at your university. Describe what the typical student does, as well as where, when, and why he/she does it. Be as specific as you can. You can use the following adverbs and connectors to enhance your report, as well as the vocabulary items listed in *Capítulo 1* of your textbook.

ADVERBIOS

comúnmente (*commonly, usually*)

siempre (*always*)

nunca (*never*)

a veces (*sometimes*)

generalmente (*generally*)

CONJUNCIONES

también (*also*)

además (*in addition*)

sin embargo (*however*)

pero (*but*)

aunque (*although*)

El estudiante típico universitario _____

_____

_____

_____

_____

_____

_____.

1-10 ¡Tus conversaciones telefónicas! Paso 1. With a classmate, write a typical telephone conversation you might have with one of the following people about your college life: your mother/father, your brother/sister, your grandparents, your aunt/uncle, your best friend, your boyfriend/girlfriend.

1. What kinds of questions does the person you chose typically ask you? What does he/she want to know about your activities?

2. Write down five questions he/she might ask.

3. Jot down your possible answers, as realistically as you can.

4. Create the dialog. Make sure you conjugate the verbs in the correct forms and use a familiar and natural conversational tone.

5. Incorporate the expressions from the dialogues in Activities 1–3 above.

Some of the expressions follow:

PEOPLE	OPENINGS	GREETINGS
mamá/papá	Bueno	Hola.
abuelo/abuela	Entonces	¿Qué tal?
tío/tía	¿Dígame?	Un beso.
novio/novia	Hola	Chao.
hermano/hermana	¡Uf!	Adiós.
mejor amigo/amiga	¡Uy¡	Hasta la próxima semana
	¡Qué va!	

Oye…

Una conversación telefónica

__: [*ring, ring*]

__: _____

__: _____

__: _____

_____

__: _____

_____

__: _____

_____

__: _____

_____

__: _____

_____

__: _____

_____

Paso 2. Now, with your classmate, read your telephone conversation aloud for the class. Can they guess with whom you are speaking? Is it a friend? A family member?

1-11 Taller creativo. There is a poetry contest for foreign language students at your university. In order to enter the contest you must write a poem of three to five lines that m contain several of the following words.

NOUNS	ADJECTIVES	VERBS	CONNECTO—
ventana	bonito/a	mirar	porque (*becau*)
mochila	favorita/a	estudiar	incluso (*even*)
residencia	excelente	llegar	también (*also*)
gente	difícil	estar	pero (*but*)
miércoles	aburrido/a	caminar	entonces (*then*)
domingo	contento/a	bailar	

Idea: Write about the beautiful things that happen when you walk to school every morning what you see, hear, smell . . .

MODELO: miércoles
   Por la mañana, miro por mi ventana favorita
   La gente camina cansada,
   El miércoles es difícil, no es bonito;
   *incluso (*even*) mi mochila está aburrida.*
   El miércoles no es mi día favorito.

Your poem must have a title! You can add a drawing that accompanies it. The best poem w be read at a student gathering.

_____

_____

_____

_____

_____

_____

   _____

Nombre: _____   **Fecha:** _____

Tu imagen (*drawing*):

ENFOQUE CULTURAL

1-12 Ciudades del mundo. You write a weekly column for the travel section of your local newspaper. This time, you are writing about traveling in Spain. Look at the pictures within the map of Spain on page 23 of your textbook. This activity can be done in groups, pairs or individually.

Paso 1. First, brainstorm on the locations highlighted in the map. What locations and offerings are pictured? Where are they located? Do you know anything else about these cities/towns? For example, what can people do in these places? Write three ideas per picture.

- _____

- _____

- _____

- _____

- _____

- _____

- _____

- _____

- _____

Paso 2. Using the ideas from *Paso 1*, write a short but enticing paragraph presenting all the good and interesting things one can do in Spain. Give a suggestive title to your column; after all, you want your audience to read your column every week!

_____

_____

_____

_____

_____

_____

_____

_____

_____

_____

CAPÍTULO

2

Mis amigos y yo

A PRIMERA VISTA

2-1   Mis amigos y yo. For this exercise you will need a recent picture of your friends (at a gathering, a baseball game, a party, etc.). If you do not have a recent picture of your friends, you can use a picture from a magazine showing a group of young people engaged in a group activity.

Paso 1. With a partner, look at the pictures and write a list of adjectives that describe four people in the pictures and their physical and personality traits. Write the name of each person at the top of the list.

PERSONA 1	PERSONA 2	PERSONA 3	PERSONA 4
Nombre: _____	Nombre: _____	Nombre: _____	Nombre: _____
_____	_____	_____	_____
_____	_____	_____	_____
_____	_____	_____	_____
_____	_____	_____	_____
_____	_____	_____	_____
_____	_____	_____	_____
_____	_____	_____	_____
_____	_____	_____	_____

Paso 2. Exchange your pictures and your list with another pair of students. You will match the people in the pictures with the adjectives written down.

2-2   Los compañeros de clase. Without revealing who it is, select a classmate and write down at least five adjectives that describe him/her. Exchange your list with a partner. Rea each other's lists and see if you can guess who it is. Select one description to read aloud t the class and see if your other classmates can guess, too.

2-3   Los colores. For this activity you will need colored labels that your teacher will provide, and a pen or pencil. With a classmate, move around the room as quickly as you c writing down the color of objects in the room (books, clothing, furniture, posters, walls, e and attaching the labels to the object. After five minutes, the pair who has placed the label correctly will win.

FUNCIONES Y FORMAS

1. Adjectives

2-4 Los objetos de la clase. Paso 1. Move around the room and find five things you would like to identify that belong to classmates. Write down the name of each object and its color (**rojo**, **azul**, etc.) or an attribute of the object (**grande**, **pequeño/a**), making sure the nouns and adjectives agree in gender and number.

MODELO: *mochila roja*

OBJETO   **COLOR**

1. _____   _____

2. _____   _____

3. _____   _____

4. _____   _____

5. _____   _____

Paso 2. Exchange your list with a classmate's. You will guess who the owner of the object is and create a sentence that describes the object and names the owner.

MODELO: Mochila roja → *La mochila roja es de Olivia.*

2. Present tense of *ser*

2-5 Las descripciones. Paso 1. With a classmate, write down on a piece of paper adjectives that best describe you both. Make two lists, one for each of you. Make sure you use the right gender!

MODELO: MARÍA: *inteligente; rubia; delgada; baja; estudiosa...*
         TÚ: *divertida; morena; delgada; baja; estudiosa...*

Paso 2. You and your classmate will introduce each other to the class or to a group of students.

MODELO: E1: *Mría es rubia. Yo soy morena. María y yo somos bajas y delgadas.*
         María es inteligente. Yo soy divertida. Las dos (both) *somos estudiosas.*

Nombre: _____   Fecha: _____

2-6 ¡Más descripciones! Paso 1. Select a famous person (movie star, musician, politici
etc.) and write down on a piece of paper adjectives that describe him or her. Make sure yo
use the right gender, and use your imagination!

MODELO: E1: *Carlos Santana es creativo y famoso. También él es mexicano.*

Paso 2. Now, get in groups of four and read your descriptions to each other to see if you a
can guess who the people are. Then discuss whether or not any of you share the same trait
to see what you all have in common with some famous people!

MODELO: E1: *Carlos Santana es simpático y guapo. Él es inteligente y trabajador.*
Y tú, ¿eres así también (also)?
E2: *Yo no soy trabajador/a, pero soy muy inteligente.*

3. *Ser* and *estar* with adjectives

2-7 Condorito y sus amigos. Paso 1. Look at the picture and describe Condorito's famil
and friends. What do they look like? What emotional state do they seem to be in? Ask a
classmate the questions.

MODELO: E1: *¿Cómo es Condorito?*
E2: *Es extraño, es alto y delgado.*
E1: *Y, ¿cómo está Condorito?*
E2: *Está contento.*

Make sure you describe the three characters in the picture.

Paso 2. Go to http://espanol.entertainment.yahoo.com/comics/condorito/amigos/index.html
to find out more about this comic strip. Describe at least two additional characters: *Ungenio*
Doña Tremebunda, Yuyito, Che Copete, etc. Which country is the comic strip *Condorito*
from? With a classmate, write a paragraph with your descriptions. Then, talk with other
classmates about the nationality of the comic strip and other additional information you
gathered.

Paso 3. Now, in groups of four, discuss with your classmates the things you have in common with—and also how you are different from—the characters you have described.

Note: If you want to know more about family relationships, review the vocabulary in *Capítulo 4: En familia,* pages 122–153.

2-8 Los adjetivos. Sopa de letras. Paso 1. Find the adjectives that describe people or things from the list below in the following puzzle.

débil	cansado	joven	fuerte
divertido	gordo	largo	delgado

L	C	O	W	Q	U	L	I	B	E	D
L	O	A	S	E	D	N	A	R	B	K
D	O	P	N	W	M	G	H	D	E	F
I	E	Y	C	S	G	D	O	F	C	T
V	M	L	N	V	A	G	Q	I	U	X
E	K	L	G	O	R	D	O	F	F	V
R	D	Q	E	A	O	R	O	U	U	J
T	H	L	L	T	D	Y	T	X	E	C
I	G	V	W	P	W	O	R	Q	R	N
D	J	C	B	A	I	A	I	U	T	J
O	Z	X	D	P	Z	J	O	V	E	N

Paso 2. Now write the adjectives in the following sentences. Pay attention to the person o
thing they refer to. The gender or number may change accordingly.

Manolo es un chico (1) _____, no es fuerte. Sin embargo (*But*) Juanita sí es
(2) _____ pero ahora está (3) _____ porque practica tenis durant
cuatro horas. Los dos son muy (4) _____; sólo tienen quince años (*fifteen yea
old*). Ellos son delgados, aunque (*although*) Manolo ahora está más (5) _____
Juanita es muy (6) _____ aunque toma un almuerzo grande todos los días.
Manolo es muy (7) _____ y simpático, no es serio. En estos momentos, es
verano (*summer*) y Juanita disfruta de (*enjoys*) unas vacaciones (8) _____.

4. Possessive adjectives

2-9 Mi compañero/a y yo. Paso 1. Read the following paragraph in which Carmen talks
about her housemate, Carolina. Fill in the blanks with the appropriate possessive adjective

(1) _____ compañera de casa se llama Carolina. Ella es de Medellín, Colombi
pero (2) _____ padres viven en Los Ángeles. Carolina tiene un novio,
Guillermo, y (3) _____ familia también es de Medellín. De hecho (*In fact*)
(4) _____ familias son amigas desde 1980. Carolina y yo nos llevamos bien (g
along), aunque nos gustan cosas diferentes. Yo soy muy organizada: (5) _____
libros y (6) _____ mochila de la universidad siempre están debajo de mi pupit
Sin embargo, las cosas de Carolina están por todas partes: ella tiene (7) _____
discos compactos en el piso, y (8) _____ ropa siempre está encima de la cama.
Cuando sale a la universidad, (9) _____ cuarto está desastroso. Pero cuando ha
una fiesta y llegan los amigos a la casa, Carolina recoge (*tidy up*) todo y
(10) _____ casa está limpia y ordenada.

Paso 2. Now answer the following questions about where you live using the appropriate possessive adjectives where necessary.

1. ¿Cómo es tu casa, tu apartamento o tu residencia estudiantil?

   _____

2. ¿Eres una persona organizada o no?

   _____

3. ¿Cómo están tu cuarto y tu casa en un día típico?

   _____

4. ¿Cómo está tu cuarto y tu casa cuando hay una ocasión especial?

   _____

5. ¿Generalmente, dónde están tus cosas—tus libros, tu mochila, etc.?

   _____

6. ¿Y tus compañeros, como están sus cuartos y donde están sus cosas usualmente?

   _____

5. Gustar

2-10 Los famosos. Think of three famous people. With your classmate, write down their names and favorite activities. Get together with another pair and impersonate these people. Your classmates will ask questions until they guess the name of the person(s).

MODELO: PAIR 1:   Sammy Sosa → béisbol
         E1, PAIR 2:   *¿Te gusta correr?*
         E1, PAIR 1:   *Sí, me gusta correr.*
         E1, PAIR 2:   *¿Te gusta jugar con una bola?*
         E1, PAIR 1:   *Sí, me gusta jugar con una bola.*
         E1, PAIR 2:   *¿Te gusta el béisbol?*
         E1, PAIR 1:   *Sí, me gusta mucho el béisbol.*
         E1, PAIR 2:   *¡Eres Sammy Sosa!*

NOMBRE   **ACTIVIDAD**

_____   _____

_____   _____

_____   _____

MOSAICOS

2-11 Taller creativo. You are a salesperson for the company Programa de transformación estético-intelectual (*"life-changing" makeover program*). Your company claims wonderful results with its special pills (*píldoras*) to change inherent characteristics and states, whether physical or emotional, into their opposites. If you are dumb, you become smart; if you are ugly, you become handsome; if you are easygoing, you become anxious; if you are thin, you become fat, etc. Your boss asks you to design a brochure in which you describe the wonders of this program. With a classmate, you will design a brochure for the program promotion.

Paso 1. Brainstorm the following ideas with your partner:

- Where the company is from and how long it company has been in business.

- The company's address, phone number, etc.

- "Testimonials" of people: tell where they are from, their age, their general traits.

For instance, Pedro Jiménez, a 34-year-old Venezuelan, is unhappy and lazy or happy and hardworking before (**antes de**) this program, but after the program, he is happy and hardworking or unhappy and lazy. Give at least two testimonials.

You may add testimonials from famous people. You must decide whether, in describing people's qualities and conditions, you need to use **ser** or **estar**.

Idea 1: _____

Idea 2: _____

Idea 3: _____

Idea 4: _____

Idea 5: _____

Idea 6: _____

Idea 7: _____

Idea 8: _____

Nombre: _____ Fecha: _____

Paso 2. Once you have the ideas, design your brochure in the space provided below or on a separate piece of paper (colored stock, for instance). Decide how the information should be organized. You can include pictures from magazines and drawings with your text to enhance the written information. (Do not allow pictures to take importance over the written text!) Your brochure must have a title and an introductory sentence that describes the program:

MODELO: *El Programa de transformación estético-intelectual es maravilloso/increíble/espectacular...*

2-12 Tu perfil. Paso 1. There will be an election for a student representative from your class. With a group of classmates, you will choose one person in your group who is charismatic and has all the qualities to win this position. Create a brochure in which you present (name, place of origin, age) the best qualities of your candidate, information about his/her likes and dislikes, and contact information. Make sure you use possessive adjectives when possible.

USEFUL WORDS

candidato	ganar	por eso
elecciones estudiantiles	ayudar	entonces
voto	luchar	
cualidades	defender	

_____

_____

_____

_____

_____

_____

_____

_____

_____

_____

_____

_____

Paso 2. Students will go around the class interviewing the candidates from each group. The they will discuss each candidate's qualities and ask each other the following questions to h determine who you would vote for.

MODELO: E1: *¿Te gusta el/la candidato/a?*
¿Qué te gusta del/de la candidato/a?
E2: *Sí, me gusta mucho él/ella.*
Me gustan sus ideas. Me gustan sus cualidades.

Otras preguntas: *¿Cómo es el/la candidato/a? ¿Cuáles son sus cualidades? ¿Crees que es sincero/a? ¿De dónde es el candidato/a?* You may also create your own questions. Who wi you vote for? Who wins?

2-13 El juego del amor. For this game you will need to form groups of four. Three of you will be "date candidates" and one of you will be the person looking for a date. You may assume any name and personality you wish. The person looking for a date will ask question of the candidates (**candidates**) and then decide which person he or she would like to take ou on a date. Before starting the game, take some time to prepare questions and to decide whicl personality traits you will assume. Follow the model.

MODELO: E1: *Candidato/a número uno, ¿Cómo eres?*
E2: *Soy guapo, inteligente y muy rico.*

ENFOQUE CULTURAL

2-14 Ciudades con presencia hispana en los Estados Unidos. Unscramble the following names of U.S. cities.

1. aiimm   _____

2. wykerno   _____

3. osnlalsgee   _____

4. gihccoa   _____

5. ntosuh   _____

2-15 Trivia. Your knowledge about Hispanics in the United States. With two classmates, answer the following questions after reading the *Enfoque cultural* section on pages 84–85 of your textbook. Do not look back at the text. See how many questions you can answer successfully!

1. Nombra un estado del medio-oeste de los Estados Unidos donde viven muchos hispanos:

_____

2. Los hispanos nacidos (*born*) en el suroeste de los Estados Unidos se llaman:

_____

3. ¿Cierto o falso? Los puertorriqueños son ciudadanos americanos desde 1848:

_____

4. ¿Cierto o falso? Todos los inmigrantes emigran a Estados Unidos para ganar más dinero:

_____

5. Un aspecto muy rico y variado de la cultura hispana es:

_____

6. ¿Cierto o falso? En Miami viven muchos puertorriqueños:

_____

7. ¿Cierto o falso? En el suroeste de los Estados Unidos la arquitectura es típicamente chilena:

_____

8. ¿Cierto o falso? "Ando brujo" significa *I have no money* entre los venezolanos:

_____

CAPÍTULO

3

El tiempo libre

A PRIMERA VISTA

3-1   El tiempo libre. Paso 1. Following the model of the readings in the *A primera vista* section on pages 90–96 of your textbook, list five things you like to do in your free time on weekends (**el fin de semana**). Then, list five things you like to do during your vacation time (**las vacaciones**) in the summer. Move about the room with your list, asking other students what they like to do in their free time. Use your list as a reference, and, if it is on your list, ask them to write their name next to your activity. Then, report to your class who likes to do the same things you like.

MODELO: el fin de semana: escuchar música
   E1: *Pedro, ¿Escuchas música los fines de semana?* or *¿Te gusta escuchar música los fines de semana?*
   E2: *Sí, escucho música los fines de semana* or *Sí, me gusta escuchar música los fines de semana.*
   E1: *¡Yo también!* or *¡A mí también me gusta! Firma aquí:* <u>Pedro</u>
   ....
   E1: [to the class] *Los fines de semana, Pedro escucha música.*

EL FIN DE SEMANA	LAS VACACIONES	¡FIRMA AQUÍ!
_____	_____	_____
_____	_____	_____
_____	_____	_____
_____	_____	_____
_____	_____	_____

Paso 2. You can elaborate with your classmates on their answers. For example, following on the **modelo** given above, ask your classmate other questions: *who, where, when,* etc.

MODELO: E1: *Oye Pedro, ¿Y con quién escuchas música?*
                    E2: *Con mi novia Caridad.*

3-2   La comida. The class will have several pictures from magazines and brochures that show appetizing meals. (At the teacher's request, you may bring in some of your own pictures.) Each picture will be given a number and displayed on the board. The class will be divided into groups. The teacher will direct each group to go to a picture and list all of the foods shown. You must write the correct definite article as well as the noun. Pay attention gender and number!

3-3   Los menús. Paso 1. The class will select several of the college or school cafeterias, dining halls, or nearby restaurants. Each group will create a menu that reflects the type of meals one can have at one of these facilities for breakfast, snacks, lunch and/or dinner. With your group, write down a menu in the box below. Make sure you specify the meal (breakfast/snack/lunch/dinner).

Paso 2. Present the menu to the other groups in the classroom. You can start your presentation with sentences such as *"Para la cena, hoy tenemos pollo con patatas."* or *"El menú completo cuesta $6.50."* With the help of the instructor, the class will discuss which menu they like better and why.

FUNCIONES Y FORMAS

1. Present tense of *hacer*, *poner*, *salir*, *traer*, and *oír*

3-4 Una excursión. You and your friends are spending the weekend in the mountains! Two of your friends (you'll give them names) discuss who will make breakfast, who will make the sandwiches for lunch, and who will complete other tasks so that you all can start your day outdoors soon! Complete the following dialog between your two friends.

Nombres:

E1: _____   E2: _____

(E1) _____: Bueno, ya estamos aquí. Ahora necesitamos decidir quién (1) _____ (hacer) las tareas de la casa esta mañana.

(E2) _____: Sí. Mira, yo siempre (2) _____ (poner) la mesa en mi casa, por eso creo que si (3) _____ (hacer) el desayuno para todos es buena idea. ¿Tú (4) _____ (poner) la mesa, entonces?

(E1) _____: De acuerdo, yo (5) _____ (poner) la mesa, y los otros (6) _____ (traer) las cosas del coche y (7) _____ (hacer) las camas.

Mientras tú (8) _____ (traer) el desayuno a la mesa y yo (9) _____ (hacer) los sándwiches para el almuerzo, nosotros (10) _____ (oír) las noticias para saber qué tiempo hace hoy en las montañas, ¿vale?

(E2) _____: Yo siempre (11) _____ (oír) la estación de la universidad cuando (12) _____ (salir) a las montañas para tener información del tiempo. Si nosotros (13) _____ (oír) las noticias del tiempo vamos a saber si hace buen tiempo hoy, (14) _____ (salir) temprano a las montañas, ¡y disfrutamos del día!

Nombre: _____   **Fecha:** _____

2. Present tense of *ir* and *ir* + *a* + infinitive

3-5 ¿Adónde vas este fin de semana? You are talking to a friend of yours about gettin
together for the weekend. Fill out the blanks with the appropriate form of the verb **ir**.

RICARDO: ¿Aló?

JULIÁN: Hola Ricardo, aquí habla Julián.

RICARDO: ¿Cómo (1) _____ las cosas? Te llamo para saber si tus hermanas Lola
Dorita (2) _____ a la fiesta de Patricia esta noche. Mis amigos Charlie
Dan, los americanos, quieren conocer a chicas peruanas y ellos ¡
(3) _____ a todas las fiestas posibles! Antes de las fiestas nosotros
siempre (4) _____ al café El Grano de Oro, junto al Museo del Or
para practicar español una o dos horas. Charlie, Dan y yo (5) _____
sobre las 7:00 de la tarde. ¿Por qué no (6) _____ al café con nosotr

JULIÁN: ¡Qué divertido! Yo puedo (7) _____ al café con vosotros, pero
mis hermanas siempre (8) _____ al cine los viernes, a la sesión
de las 7:20 de la tarde con unos vecinos (*neighbors*). ¿Qué tal si nosotros
(9) _____ a la puerta del cine a las 9:00? Así ellas
(10) _____ al cine, y vosotros (11) _____ al café, com
siempre. De allí, podemos (12) _____ todos juntos a la fiesta.

3-6 Los planes. Paso 1. Make a list of things college students typically do on weekends. Then, go around the room asking your classmates whether or not they will do any of these things during the coming weekend. If they do, make sure you have them sign your name on your list.

MODELO: Ir al cine
Tocar un instrumento musical
E1: *¿Vas a tocar un instrumento musical este fin de semana?*
E2: *Sí, de hecho* (in fact) *voy a tocar en una banda de música.*
E1: *¡Firma aquí, por favor!* <u>*Jessica / Sean*</u>

ACTIVIDAD	FIRMA AQUÍ
_____	_____
_____	_____
_____	_____
_____	_____
_____	_____
_____	_____
_____	_____
_____	_____
_____	_____

Paso 2. Now, report to your class, or to a group of classmates, who is going to do what this weekend.

MODELO: *Sean y Jessica van a tocar en una banda de música.*
Daniel y yo vamos a ir a ver "Las Horas" a la sesión de las 7:00 de la tarde.

3-7 Una agenda ocupada. You are trying to arrange a date with a friend, but she is very busy. Fill in the blanks with the best verb possible from the list below.

beber	comer	descansar	leer	terminar	tomar el sol
cenar	deber	escribir	nadar	tocar	ver

TÚ: Hola Julieta. ¡El miércoles por fin (1) _____ las clases y comienz_ el descanso de otoño! Venga, Julieta, vamos a vernos el jueves, ¿te parece bien?

JULIETA: Es que (It's just that) no sé . . . El jueves por la tarde nosotros (2) _____ a visitar a mi abuela en la residencia de ancianos (senior citizen). Además, antes de esto, (3) _____ una carta para un trab_ de verano en mi ciudad.

TÚ: A ver… el viernes yo (4) _____ con Pascual en el restaurante "L_ dos Amigos" a las 9:00 de la noche, pero después él (5) _____ e_ la banda de jazz en el bar "Todojazz". ¿Qué tal si (6) _____ unas cervezas allí?

JULIETA: Es que el viernes mi hermano Juan, su amigo Charlie y yo (7) _____ una película en su casa. Además, el sábado por la mañana Araceli y yo (8) _____ en la playa del Ahogado. ¿Por qué no (9) _____ con nosotras en el mar?

TÚ: Me parece bien. Es muy difícil poder salir contigo, Julieta, así que el sábado por la mañana es la única solución. . . . Te (10) _____ el sábado en la playa del Ahogado entonces.

3. Numbers 100 to 2,000,000

3-8 La población hispana. Look for the following information on http://peru.gotolatin.com/spa/Info/Hbook/basicdata.asp under the link sections "Datos básicos." Then, report your results to the class. Make sure you read the numbers aloud. Write them in numbers and letters.

1. ¿Cuál es la superficie total del país, en kilómetros cuadrados (kms^2)?

   _____

2. ¿Cuál es la población total de Perú?

   _____

3. ¿Cuántos habitantes tiene la ciudad de Lima?

   _____

4. ¿Cuántos distritos hay en Lima?

   _____

5. Cuántos idiomas oficiales hay en el país? ¿Cuáles son?

   _____

3-9 Qué pasó y cuándo. Match the following dates with the events. Then, think of two events in United States history, or at your college or university (when it was founded, for example), and have your classmates give the date aloud to the class.

1. 711   **a.** Llegan los árabes a la Península Ibérica (España y Portugal).

2. 1939   **b.** Cristobal Colón llega al continente americano.

3. 1492   **c.** Los estadounidenses re-eligen a George W. Bush como presidente.

4. 2001   **d.** Hay un ataque terrorista en las Torres Gemelas.

5. 2004   **f.** Termina la Segunda Guerra Mundial.

6. ?   **g.** _____

7. ?   **h.** _____

3-10 ¡A ganar la lotería! Your teacher will give you a piece of paper with a number from 100 to 2,000,000 written on it. Write out the number—in words—in Spanish on a separate piece of paper. When you are done writing out the number, hand back the piece of paper your teacher originally gave you. Your teacher will put all the numbers together and will ask a student to draw one of the numbers and read it aloud. Whoever has the number that is drawn will win, but only if it is written correctly! Make sure that you understand how to say your number so that you will recognize it if it is the winning number.

4. *Saber* and *conocer*

3-11 Las películas. Write a list of three recent well-known movies. Next, write a list of questions about these movies: the plot, the actors, the theme/subject, and where you can go see them. Decide whether to use **saber** or **conocer** in your questions. Ask a classmate or a group of classmates the questions you have prepared. They should answer accordingly, using **saber** and **conocer**.

Películas

1. _____

2. _____

3. _____

Preguntas

1. _____

2. _____

3. _____

3-12 Personas famosas. Do you know any famous people? If so, whom? If not, who would you like to know? Write down the names of three famous people. Then, in Spanish, write if you know them and at least two things you know about them. Decide whether to use **saber** or **conocer** in your sentences.

Persona famosa 1: _____

Persona famosa 2: _____

Persona famosa 3: _____

3-13 Soy experto/a. What are some subjects on which you would consider yourself an "expert"? A certain type of music? A certain sport? Write down in Spanish the name of the subject you know and at least three things you know about it. Decide whether to use **saber** or **conocer** in your sentences.

Soy experto en:

Tres cosas sobre _____ :

1. _____

2. _____

3. _____

Now move around the room and ask your classmates what subjects they know well and what they know about them. Is there anyone who is an "expert" in the same subject as you?

5. Some uses of *por* and *para*

3-14 ¿Por o para? Paso 1. Decide whether you use **por** or **para** for the following phrases and situations.

1. A Manuela no le gusta hablar _____ teléfono.

2. Una actividad interesante es, _____ ejemplo, ver películas clásicas.

3. Camino _____ el parque todos los días.

4. Debes comer bien _____ no estar enfermo.

5. Juan y Manuela compran los libros _____ la clase de biología.

6. El tren sale _____ Cuzco a las tres de la tarde.

7. El tren viaja a Cuzco _____ lugares verdes y muy hermosos.

8. Vamos a visitar Cuzco _____ tres días.

Paso 2. Now, adapting these situations to your own likes, dislikes, and activities, write down five sentences in which you use the prepositions **por** and **para** in a meaningful and personal manner: Do you like to talk on the phone? Where do you walk every day? What is your next destination? How long will you be there? etc.

_____

_____

_____

_____

_____

MOSAICOS

3-15 Taller creativo. Julieta receives a phone message on her cell phone from her grandm▪
Julia, who lives at a senior citizen center. She is worried about her boyfriend, Pedro, and ɑ
Julieta to write him an e-mail with advice. What should Julieta tell Pedro? Use **deber** to
advise Pedro. Here is the phone message:

> Hola Julieta, soy abuela. Te llamo porque Pedro, mi novio, está enfermo y yo estoy
> preocupada. Pedro no come bien y creo (*I think*) que está deprimido. No sale de su
> habitación, y los médicos dicen que está deshidratado. Sólo ve televisión y no habla co▪
> sus amigos, ni juega (*play*) dominó los domingos. Tampoco camina mucho, así que es▪
> débil, no va al gimnasio ni a la piscina. Por favor, escribe un mensaje electrónico a Peᴅ
> con tu consejo (*advice*). Él siempre te escucha, tú eres joven y lista. Cenamos a las 7:0▪
> de la tarde, pero Pedro y yo vamos a estar en la sala de computadoras hasta las 6:30.
> Debes envíar una copia (cc) a mi dirección. Espero tu respuesta. Un beso muy fuerte.
> Abuela Julia.

De: _____

A: _____

RE: _____

CC: _____

Querido Pedro:

_____
_____
_____
_____
_____
_____
_____
_____
_____

Hasta pronto

_____

Nombre: _____   Fecha: _____ ■

3-16 Buscapalabras. You got a virus in your e-mail and have received the following unreadable message. It is important that you decipher the message, since you must meet your friend Gustavo who is arriving from Lima, Perú, tomorrow, and who has no other way of communicating with you. Circle the words and then write them on the lines provided. Read the text to another classmate to make sure you got the message. Hint: The first words in the message are "LLEGO" and "A."

XCV¡URGENTE!QPL

LLEGOMVKSAMSVNLASVMSKSDOCEMVSPODYVVBKMEDIAVMSKENVMDS

UNVMDAVIÓNMVSPDESDEVKLIMAMVPSAMIAMI.MVPODESDEVDSMIAMIM

VIEWVOYVMPAMVISTOMARMVUNMPOWAUTOBÚSVSLVHASTAMVSTUMV

DPUNIVERSIDAD.MVPCALCULOMVOPQUEVMIPVOYMVPIAMVOPESTARMV

PIENTUMWUNIVERSIDADMIWELMVIWOVIERNESMIOPORMIOLACVTARDE.

NECESITOMVIOWVERMVWALMPOIPROFESORMVIOWRAMIREZMVIOPARA

MVIUNVNTRABAJOVMWODEMLKPVERANO.MIODEBESMIOLLAMARMIOAM

IOWSUNIUWOFICINA,MIOPORVVWIFAVOR,VNWYWEOPEDIRUNAWENCITA

VNWUPARAWEUMÍ.VWTAMBIÉNWBEDEBESEIWUPRESENTARMEWIEANBO

IWJULIETA,WLKMEUWIWGUSTAMEPEMUCHOWOEISUWOEIFOTO,LWYETD

ESEOMWTHABLARWELKCONMWELLA.¿VAMOSMWIEAEFCENARWELKCON

SDVNJULIETA?VPW¡DEBESVNAWESTARWEOAWOUFEOWGLASWEPICINCO

EUGDEQLKLARWIYTARDEVNWENWFLAWEFNESTACIÓN!WE

MPSALUDOS,MOWGUSTAVOPOXZ

ENFOQUE CULTURAL

3-17 Un viaje al Perú de los Incas. Julieta's grandmother is planning to take her friends at the senior citizen center on a ten-day trip to Perú to celebrate her sixty-eighth birthday (she is in optimal health!). She is savvy in surfing the Net and has found a couple of good websites, but does not speak Spanish, so she is asking Julieta and her friends to help her with the plans for the trip to send to her travel agent.

Your group and you are going to plan the entire ten-day trip for Julieta's grandmother and her four friends. You must give them advice and tell them where they are going to go, what sightseeing they must do, and the places of interest they must not miss. Using a map of Perú, the information presented in the *Enfoque Cultural* section on pages 118–119 of your textbook, and the following websites, you will give these energetic ladies a ten-day trip packed with interesting activities. You must include information such as dates of departure from and arrivals to different cities, things to carry, nightlife, restaurants to go to, typical meals to eat, famous monuments and sights, and any other imaginable aspect to make their trip a once in a lifetime event.

URLs:

http://www.peru.info/peru.asp

http://www.peruturismo.com

Día 1:

_____

_____

_____

Día 2:

_____

_____

_____

Día 3:

_____

_____

_____

Nombre: _____   Fecha: _____

Día 4:

_____

_____

_____

Día 5:

_____

_____

_____

Día 6:

_____

_____

_____

Día 7:

_____

_____

_____

Día 8:

_____

_____

_____

Día 9:

_____

_____

_____

Día 10:

_____

_____

_____

CAPÍTULO

4

En familia

A PRIMERA VISTA

4-1 Imagina... Imagine that you had been born into a Hispanic family. What would likely be the names of your parents, your siblings, your grandparents? For example, if your father is John Gardner and your mother is Julie (maiden name: Smith), their names could be, respectively, Juan García and Julia Sánchez. What would be your mother's maiden name? How would you combine your parents' last names? What would be your last name?

Paso 1. Create your Hispanic family tree. Make sure you follow the rules of name giving presented on pages 124–125 of the *A primera vista* section of your textbook. Read the *Lengua* and *Cultura* boxes in this section.

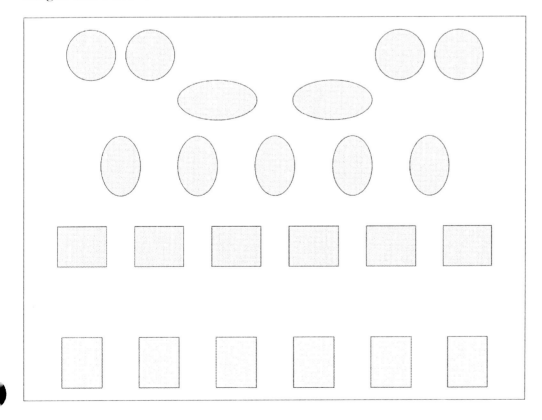

Paso 2. Describe your family tree to your classmate. Explain who's who, how they're rel
to you, and give their full name. Isn't it fun (and complex) to be part of a Hispanic family

4-2 La familia de Julieta. Julieta has asked you to help her with her big graduation
weekend. You need to pick up her relatives at the airport, but who's who in this list?

Paso 1. Try to solve the mystery by identifying these people's relationships to Julieta.

Note: (h) hombre; (m) mujer

Tu amiga: Julieta Escartín Molina

1. Joaquín Escartín Segovia (h)   _____ de Julieta

2. Eugenia Molina Segura (m)   _____ de Julieta

3. José Pedro Escartín Molina (h)   _____ de Julieta

4. Valeria Escartín Molina (m)   _____ de Julieta

5. Vicente Molina Segura (h)   _____ de Julieta

6. Mónica Molina Blanco (m)   _____ de Julieta

7. Julián Molina Blanco (h)   _____ de Julieta

8. Eulalia Blanco Bernal (m)   _____ de Julieta

Paso 2. Now, according to the information above, identify the relationships of these people
to Vicente Molina Segura, one of Julieta's relatives.

Vicente Molina Segura

1. Julieta Escartín Molina (m)   _____ de Vicente

2. Eugenia Molina Segura (m)   _____ de Vicente

3. José Pedro Escartín Molina (h)   _____ de Vicente

4. Valeria Escartín Molina (m)   _____ de Vicente

5. Eulalia Blanco Bernal (m)   _____ de Vicente

6. Mónica Molina Blanco (m)   _____ de Vicente

7. Julián Molina Blanco (h)   _____ de Vicente

8. Joaquín Escartín Segovia (h)   _____ de Vicente

4-3 Los SuperGarcía. The García family is an amazing bunch. This family is nothing like an ordinary family. It is composed of many siblings, grandparents, and pets. They all have special traits that make them unusual, such as their names, the places they travel, the games they like to play, and their lives in general are extraordinary.

Paso 1. With a classmate, invent a family tree for this family: Los SuperGarcía, superhéroes del barrio (*The SuperGarcía family, the superheroes of the neighborhood*).

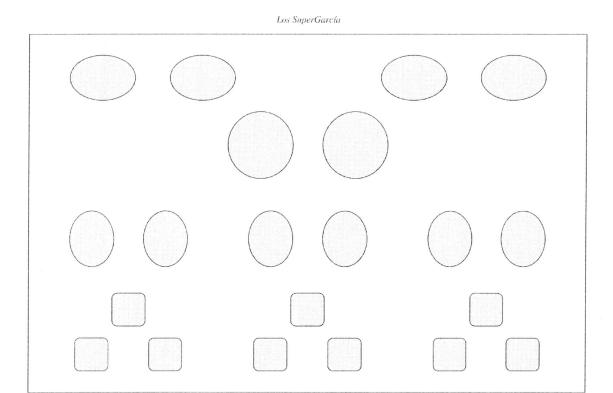

Los SuperGarcía

Paso 2. Now write their activities, their preferences, what they do, etc. You can follow the format of the reading "¿Qué hacen los parientes?" on page 127 of your textbook.

Los SuperGarcía, Superhéroes del Barrio

_____

_____

_____

_____

_____

_____

_____

_____

_____

_____

_____

_____

_____

_____

_____

_____

_____

FUNCIONES Y FORMAS

1. Present tense of stem-changing verbs (*e → ie, o → ue, e → i*)

4-4 El fin de semana. You are part of a group of students going away to the mountains for the weekend. You will pack food, sports equipment, music, and other things you will need for your trip. In order to make a list of things to pack, you first need to know your preferences: your favorite sports, your favorite foods, etc.

Paso 1. Make a list of the things you like to eat, the sports you play, the music you prefer to listen to, and the things you plan (**pensar**) to do during the weekend.

COMIDAS	MÚSICA	DEPORTES	PLANES Y ACTIVIDADES
_____	_____	_____	_____
_____	_____	_____	_____
_____	_____	_____	_____
_____	_____	_____	_____
_____	_____	_____	_____
_____	_____	_____	_____
_____	_____	_____	_____
_____	_____	_____	_____

Paso 2. Now, with the group of students, compare your lists.

MODELO: E1: *Yo prefiero tomar cereal por la mañana.*
  E2: *Yo sólo como fruta por la mañana.*
  E3: *Me gusta el cereal con fruta. Entonces, ¿llevamos cereales y fruta?*
  E1 y E2: *¡De acuerdo!*

Make sure you use as many verbs as possible from the list of verbs in *Funciones y formas* in your textbook on page 133.

4-5   Una entrevista. With a classmate, create a number of questions to use to interview y____
teacher.

Paso 1. First, list the questions you would ask your teacher about his or her regular activi____
family, daily schedule, plans, preferences, etc. If you wish, base your questions on the
information from Activities 4-3 and 4-4. Then, ask your teacher the questions. You can st____
your interview in the following manner:

MODELO: *Profesora, yo prefiero tomar cereal para el desayuno, pero mi compañero/a c____*
          fruta. Y usted, ¿qué prefiere comer por la mañana?

          or:

          Profesora, mi compañero sale de casa a las 8:00 y yo salgo a las 8:10. Y usted
          ¿a qué hora sale de su casa por las mañanas?

Paso 2. Then, with a classmate, write a brief account of your teacher's activities in the box
below:

MI PROFESOR/A
_____
_____
_____
_____
_____
_____
_____
_____
_____
_____
_____
_____
_____
_____
_____
_____
_____

2. *Tener que + infinitive.*

4-6 Responsabilidades. Paso 1. Make a list of the five most important things that you have to do at school or work on a weekly basis. Use **tener que + infinitive** to indicate what you have to do.

MODELO: mi clase de química → *Tengo que ir al laboratorio.*
        Mis responsabilidades semanales:

QUÉ O DÓNDE   **RESPONSABILIDAD**

_____   _____

_____   _____

_____   _____

_____   _____

_____   _____

Paso 2. Work with a classmate, and, based on what you wrote down in Paso 1, ask each other what you have to do every week. What responsibilities do you have in common? What responsibilities are different?

3. Adverbs

4-7 En invierno y en verano. Paso 1. Make a list of activities you often do (or do not do) in winter and summer.

Actividades

_____

_____

_____

_____

_____

_____

_____

_____

Paso 2. Get together with a classmate and discuss how you go about your activities in different seasons, using adverbs.

MODELO: desayunar
     E1: *En invierno yo no desayuno generalmente, porque salgo muy temprano de casa, pero en verano yo desayuno frecuentemente.*
     E2: *Sí, en invierno yo desayuno rápidamente, pero en verano, desayuno lentamente, con cereales, café y jugo.*

Paso 3. Now think of activities you and a member of your family do often. Compare his o~~r~~ her way of doing these activities with your way.

MODELO: pasear
     E1: *Mi abuelo pasea por el parque frecuentemente, pero yo no paseo, generalmente.*
     E2: *Sí, mi abuelo también pasea, pero él pasea lentamente y yo paseo rápidamente.*

4. *Hace* with expressions of time

4-8 Para conocernos. Paso 1. Write a list of your accomplishments: the sports you play, musical instruments you play, activities, hobbies, or any other personal accomplishments y~~ou~~ feel proud of.

ACTIVIDADES

_____

_____

_____

_____

_____

_____

_____

_____

_____

_____

Paso 2. Exchange your list with that of your classmate, and ask each other how long you have been doing each activity.

MODELO: E1: *Escribir poesía.*
  E2: *¿Cuánto tiempo hace que escribes poesía?*
  E1: *Hace dos años que escribo poesía.*

5. Reflexive verbs and pronouns

4-9 Encuesta. Using the following reflexive verbs, move around the class, asking your classmates if they do these things and in which order they do them. Make sure they sign their names.

	ANTES DE DESAYUNAR	DESPUÉS DE DESAYUNAR	NUNCA	FIRMA AQUÍ
Se levanta				
Se baña				
Se peina				
Se seca				
Se viste				

Now, find similarities between your classmates and yourself.

MODELO: *Yo me peino antes de desayunar, y Carlos también* (also).

or:

Mariana no se peina nunca, y yo tampoco (neither).

MOSAICOS

4-10 Cuentos de hadas. Paso 1. Complete the following passages. Then identify the fair
tale (**cuento de hadas**) that matches the description.

I

Su madrastra no (1) _____ (poner) la mesa.

Sus hermanastras (2) _____ (levantarse) muy tarde todos los días.

Ella (3) _____ (vestirse) con ropas viejas.

El príncipe (4) _____ (querer) encontrar a la mujer del zapato de cristal.

Ella siempre (5) _____ (hacer) las camas, y el desayuno.

¿Cómo se llama el cuento?

II

Ella (1) _____ (salir) de su casa todas las tardes y (2) _____ (llevar)
una cestita con comida a su abuelita.

Su abuelita (3) _____ (dormir) todo el día.

El lobo (4) _____ (querer) comerse a la abuelita.

El cazador (5) _____ (vestirse) con la ropa de la abuelita.

¿Cómo se llama el cuento?

Paso 2. Now, create your own fill-in-the-blank story. With a classmate, think of a well-
known children's tale and write five to eight sentences like those in I and II. Then, exchang
stories with another student pair. You will complete each other's story and then guess the
name of it.

1. _____

2. _____

3. _____

4. _____

5. _____

6. _____

7. _____

8. _____

¿Cómo se llama el cuento? _____

4-11 La fiesta de Julieta. Complete the story of Julieta's graduation party preparations.

1. Mónica _____ (poner) los platos y los vasos en las mesas.

2. Julián _____ (jugar) al béisbol y al tenis con los vecinos de Julieta; él es muy joven y no ayuda con los preparativos.

3. El papá de Julieta _____ (traer) las bebidas de la tienda.

4. El abuelo de Julieta _____ (dormir) en el sofá porque es viejo y está cansado.

5. La tía Eulalia y la abuelita _____ (oir) las noticias en la radio.

6. Su hermano José Pedro y su mamá _____ (hacer) los sándwiches.

7. El tío de Julieta _____ (servir) los refrescos a los amigos de Julieta.

8. Valeria, la hermana de Julieta, _____ (leer) el periódico.

Enfoque cultural

4-12 Una carta. You are spending two weeks with a family in Colombia, and visiting the cities of Bogotá, Medellín, and Cartagena. Use the information from *Enfoque cultural* on pages 150–151 of your textbook. You can also research using the Internet. (Some useful sites are: http://www.colombia.com/turismo/ and http://www.colombianparadise.com/.) You will write a letter in Spanish to your family members (so they can appreciate your linguistic progress) describing the activities you do while you are in each city, describing their location (mountain, coast), history, attractions, etc. You are learning cultural aspects as well, such as music and dance, family traditions, and even certain idioms you have incorporated into your everyday vocabulary!

Make sure you begin your letter appropriately:

Querido/Querida/Queridos/Queridas

And make sure that you say good-bye:

Con cariño / Un saludo / Un abrazo / Te quiere tu hijo/a

CAPÍTULO

5

Mi casa es su casa

A PRIMERA VISTA

5-1   De tiendas. Make a list of some of the furniture and appliances that are sold in stores where you live. Then, read the list to a classmate, who will have to guess the name(s) of the store(s).

MODELO: Vendemos computadoras, cámaras de video, televisores, radios y equipos de música.
Tienda → Best Buy

LISTA	TIENDA
_____	_____
_____	_____
_____	_____
_____	_____
_____	_____
_____	_____
_____	_____
_____	_____

5-2 Tu casa ideal. Look for pictures of rooms, bathrooms, kitchens, as well as househol[...]
items (linens, bedding, etc.) in magazines and newspapers, and bring them to class. In gro[...]
of four, draw your "ideal" house on the chalkboard, placing the pictures on the board to s[...]
your design of the house. Write the names of the rooms and the items each room holds. T[...]
present your ideal house orally to the rest of your classmates. Make sure you describe eac[...]
room and the items in it. The whole class will vote for the best "ideal" house!

5-3 Anuncios inmobiliarios. Paso 1. Grupo A: Your classmate and you are looking for [...]
apartment for the next academic term. Write an advertisement in which you describe the t[...]
of apartment you want to rent: number of rooms, appliances, furniture you will need, etc.
You must also give an estimated price you are willing to pay per month.

Grupo B: You and your classmate are subletting your apartment for the next academic term. Write a classified ad in which you advertise your apartment: number of rooms, appliances included, and type of furniture it has. You must also give an estimated rental cost.

_____

Paso 2.

Exchange your ad with that of the other group. Find out more about the apartment, describe your needs and your conditions, and try to reach an agreement with the other party.

FUNCIONES Y FORMAS

1. Present progressive

5-4   Al otro lado del Atlántico.

Estudiante A: Your best friend is spending a semester abroad in Salamanca, Spain. It is 6:00 p.m. in your town in the United States and 12:00 a.m. in Salamanca. You write your friend an e-mail inquiring about his or her activities. What is he or she doing right now? Y also describe what you are doing. You ask your friend to write back immediately. Estudia B: You are spending a semester abroad in Salamanca, Spain. It is midnight in Salamanca a you've just received an e-mail from your best friend, in which he or she tells you what he she is doing at the moment, and inquires about your current activities. Respond to the message.

(Note to the teacher: This exercise can be done at the language lab, as an on-line chat activity).

```
Para:     _____@_____

De:       _____@_____

RE:       _____

-------------------------------------------------------------------
_____

_____

_____

_____

_____

_____
```

5-5. ¿Qué estás haciendo? Paso 1. Your instructor will provide you with magazine photos from home magazines that portray houses, rooms, and furniture. (Your teacher may suggest that you look for your own photos to bring to class.) Look at the pictures and imagine that you are in each picture, and write sentences indicating what you are doing in each one. For example, if you have a picture of a kitchen, you might write "Estoy preparando la cena para mis amigos."

Paso 2. Form groups of three and, without sharing what you have written, show your pictures to each other. Each of you should ask questions to find out what your classmates are doing in each picture. Indicate whether your classmates guessed right!

2. Expressions with *tener*

5-6   Sopa de letras. Paso 1. Find the noun that describes the emotions and states listed below. Then write each one in the correct space below.

W	E	R	A	Z	O	N	Y	C	U	F
D	T	M	O	S	D	M	K	A	F	D
B	G	F	A	F	E	H	J	L	P	L
X	N	Q	O	A	I	D	F	O	K	R
V	R	I	P	Ñ	M	C	E	R	E	W
C	O	H	R	Q	E	Z	T	Q	I	P
Y	T	F	I	U	J	U	L	J	Y	O
E	O	L	S	N	F	J	S	P	K	L
P	K	H	A	M	B	R	E	R	B	D
R	S	F	D	M	U	G	D	U	P	H
N	P	G	F	X	E	G	E	W	E	Q

1. _____ Necesitas beber agua.

2. _____ Es invierno y no llevas un suéter.

3. _____ Son las tres de la tarde y no tienes dinero para el almuerzo.

4. _____ ¡Te levantas a las 8:45 de la mañana y tu clase comienza a las 9:00 de la mañana!

5. _____ Es de noche, y un animal enorme camina hacia ti rápidamente.

6. _____ Estás muy cansado y necesitas irte a la cama pronto.

7. _____ Es verano y estás trabajando en el jardín.

8. _____ Conoces la verdad y dices la información correcta.

Paso 2. Now, write eight questions for your classmates about the emotions and states listed on the previous page.

MODELO: E1: *¿Cuándo tienes suerte?*
E2: *¡Tengo suerte cuando una chica / un chico me llama para ir al cine!*

3. Direct object nouns and pronouns

5-7 La casa Co-op.

Estudiante 1: You are still looking for a place to live during the next academic year! Your friend, who lives in a Hispanic student co-op house, invites you to visit it and inquire. Each student must do different chores to keep the house clean and running, and you ask your friend about each person's responsibilities. Write down your questions. Then, ask your classmate. He or she must answer accordingly.

Estudiante 2: Your friend is looking for a place to live, and your co-op house has an opening. You invite him or her to visit and ask questions about people's chores and responsibilities. Using the chart below, decide what each person in your co-op does and when. You will answer your friend's questions.

MODELO: E1: *¿Quién limpia el cuarto de baño?*
E2: *Cecilia lo limpia los lunes y yo lo limpio los jueves.*

Make sure you use the correct direct object pronouns in your answers.

ESTUDIANTES	TAREAS DE LA CASA	DÍAS DE LA SEMANA
Julio	lavar la ropa	lunes
Mariano	doblar la ropa	martes
Alberto	preparar la cena	miércoles
Macarena	sacar la basura	jueves
Alicia	hacer las camas	viernes
Fernando	barrer el piso	sábado
Maria Luisa	lavar los platos	domingo
Cecilia	limpiar el cuarto de baño	lunes
?...	?...	?...
?...	?...	?...

5-8   Examen de personalidad. Are you a responsible person? Are you lazy? Are you absentminded?

Paso 1. Check one of the options for each situation, and then answer each question your classmate will ask, using direct object pronouns.

	SIEMPRE 3	A VECES 2	NUNCA 1
Hacer la cama			
Planchar las camisas (*shirts*)			
Lavar y secar los platos			
Preparar el almuerzo			
Pasar la aspiradora al piso			
Hablar con mis abuelos			
Llamar a mis familiares en su cumpleaños			
Doblar la ropa interior (*underwear*)			

MODELO: E1: *¿Haces la cama siempre?*
          E2: *Sí, yo siempre la hago por la mañana. / No, no la hago nunca. / La hago a veces, cuando me visitan mis amigos.*

Paso 2. Now check the number of points you got with the chart below and give the reasons for your test results to your classmate or to the entire class.

Puntos:

A. 6–12: Definitivamente, no te gustan las tareas de la casa. Aunque amas a tu familia, no consideras estas responsabilidades demasiado importantes. Eres más bien perezoso/a. Debes intentar ser más activo/a y diligente.

B. 12–18: Bueno, eres algo perezoso/a. Te gusta el orden pero no te preocupa demasiado, porque eres una persona ocupada y algo despistada (*absent-minded*). Las tareas de la casa no son tu prioridad, pero con disciplina puedes ser un/a buen/a compañero/a de cuarto.

C. 18–24: ¡Eres un/a excelente compañero/a de cuarto! Eres disciplinado/a, diligente y activo/a. Te preocupas por los familiares y eres responsable. Tus amigos te admiran por estas cualidades.

¿Qué tipo eres tú?

4. Demonstrative adjectives and pronouns

5-9   La mudanza. Find different pictures of pieces of furniture and have them at hand. Imagine that you are helping a friend to move into his or her new apartment. You will ask your friend where to place each item. Your friend will answer accordingly.

MODELO: E1: *¿Dónde ponemos/pongo estas mesas?*
E2: *Debes ponerlas aquí. / Ésta debes ponerla en la cocina, y aquélla en el sal*

MOSAICOS

5-10 Taller creativo: Un poema. You and your friend are desperate to have your roommates do their chores every day of the week. You have decided to write a poem to recite every morning, so that everybody does their chores! You have the beginning and the end of the poem as models below. Write the rest of the days' chores. Saturdays and Sundays are your days off.

You can write your poems on construction paper and present them to the whole class.

Poema

Título: _____

Los lunes siempre limpiamos el baño:

Aunque tenemos mucho trabajo,

¡lo limpiamos más de una vez al año!

Los martes . . . _____

_____

_____

Los miércoles . . . _____

_____

_____

Los jueves . . . _____

_____

_____

Los viernes . . . _____

_____

_____

Los sábados y los domingos descansamos;

durante el fin de semana, vienen los amigos y bailamos.

¡Por eso el lunes, otra vez las tareas de la casa comenzamos!

ENFOQUE CULTURAL

5-11 Latin-trivia. As part of the preparation for this activity, you will find basic informa about the three countries presented in *Enfoque cultural* on pages 184–185 of your textboo You will find more information on the website www.guiadelmundo.com, under Centroamérica → Honduras, El Salvador, and Nicaragua, in various information sections each country.

Paso 1. With a classmate, write twelve questions using the information you have gathered from the website above.

Preguntas:

Nicaragua

1. ¿_____

2. ¿_____

3. ¿_____

4. ¿_____

El Salvador

1. ¿_____

2. ¿_____

3. ¿_____

4. ¿_____

Honduras

1. ¿_____

2. ¿_____

3. ¿_____

4. ¿_____

Paso 2. With your classmate, prepare a prize for this trivia contest. The prize must consist of a household item, furniture, or appliance. Write a list of the items included in the prize (for example, a set of living room furniture; make sure you give details).

Premio: _____

Artículos incluídos:

_____, _____, _____

_____, _____, _____

Paso 3. Now, pose your questions to a group of students (at least two other pairs) in the classroom or to all the students in the classroom. The pair who answers the most questions correctly will win your prize. You must present the prize to this pair in front of the class.

De compras

A PRIMERA VISTA

6-1 Consejos de guardarropa. Paso 1. Using your knowledge of the Spanish-speaking world, your textbook maps, and information in the *Enfoque cultural* sections, your partner and you will make a list of five different places in the Spanish-speaking world you would like to visit. Make sure that the places include both rural and urban areas, different climates and/or seasons of the year, and different geographical aspects. Decide how you'd spend the time: walking, sightseeing, shopping, visiting museums, etc. Exchange your list with that of another pair.

LUGAR	CLIMA Y TEMPORADA	ACTIVIDAD
_____	_____	_____
_____	_____	_____
_____	_____	_____
_____	_____	_____
_____	_____	_____

Paso 2. You will decide on the type of clothing your friends will need to wear based on tℏ list. Write a paragraph with your advice.

MODELO: PAREJA 1: *Lugar   Clima y temporada   Actividad*
                        Pirineos   Montaña--mayo   Turismo por parques nacionales eⁿ
                                                          bicicleta

        PAREJA 2: *Para hacer turismo en bicicleta por los Pirineos en el mes de mayᵒ*
        necesitan dos pantalones de algodón, dos camisetas, ropa interior, un
        impermeable para la lluvia, unas botas de caminar y un suéter de lana.

6-2   ¿Quién es? Choose a classmate and, without writing down or revealing his or her naⁿ write a detailed description of what he or she is wearing. Read your description aloud to tℏ class to see if your classmates can guess who it is!

6-3   Mercados multiculturales. The class will create a Hispanic flea market! The class wᵢ divide into two groups: sellers (**vendedores**) and buyers (**clientes**). Students will provide clothing and accessories for the stands. You can also use pictures from magazines and newspapers.

Vendedores: Sellers (one or two students per stand) will set up market stands with clothes and accessories for others to buy. You will decide on the price of your articles (in bolívares and tag them. Your buyers will have 100,000 bolívares to spend on items.

Clientes: In pairs or groups of three, you will walk around the market, buying and bargainⁱ (regatear) with the sellers. You have 100,000 bolívares to spend. After shopping, students will present their purchases and the money spent on them.

NOTE: Before you start the activity, make sure you review the dialogue in *De compras* on pages 191–192 of your textbook.

Palabras y frases útiles:

    probarse   gastar

    cambiar   quedarle/me/te bien

    pagar   quedar

¿En qué puedo ayudarle/servirle?

    Quisiera …

    Me gustaría …

FUNCIONES Y FORMAS

1. Preterit tense of regular verbs

6-4   Reporteros del mundo. Think of some actions of celebrities that happened in the last few weeks or months in your country or in the world. Now, with your classmate present a brief news report on these issues. Use verbs studied in the chapter in the preterit tense when reporting on these people's activities.

Noticias

1. _____

   _____

2. _____

   _____

3. _____

   _____

4. _____

   _____

5. _____

   _____

6-5   ¿Qué llevaron los famosos? Look for celebrity photos from magazines that show stars at different events and outings. Bring the photos to class and, working in groups of three or four, tell your classmates what the celebrities wore to the events, where they went, how much they paid for the clothing, etc. You may use the following verbs: **ponerse, llevar, pagar, gastar, quedar**.

2. Preterit of *ir* and *ser*

6-6   Tu minuto de oro. Using the preterit of **ser** and **ir**, each student will have 30 seconds to tell a classmate about an important event he or she participated in when it was (date), where he/she went, what it was like. The other person will tell a group of students his or her classmate's story.

MODELO: E1: Fue el 6 de mayo de 2004. Yo fui a conocer el país de Venezuela. Fui a Isl Margarita, y a la capital, Caracas. Fue un viaje inolvidable porque fue la primera vez que fui al extranjero solo.

E2: Fue el 6 de mayo de 2004. Él fue a conocer el país de Venezuela. Fue a Isl Margarita, y a la capital, Caracas. Fue un viaje inolvidable porque fue la primera vez que él/ella fue al extranjero solo.

3. Indirect object nouns and pronouns

6-7 Examen de personalidad. Answer the following questions and find out your personality type: Are you a generous person? What acts of generosity do you perform? Th compare your answers with your classmate's. Write a report on your classmate's acts of generosity.

Say what you would do in the following situations.

MODELO: ¿Qué haces . . . ?
Si un amigo te pide tu tarjeta de crédito:
A. *Le doy dinero.* Or:
B. *¡No le doy dinero y tampoco (either) le presto la tarjeta de crédito!*
¿Qué haces . . . ?

1. Si tu hermano tiene una cita a ciegas (*blind date*) y necesita un traje y una corbata elegantes: _____

2. Si una viejita te pide llevar sus bolsas de la compra: _____

3. Si yo quiero hacer una fiesta de cumpleaños: _____

4. Si tu amigo/a no sabe cocinar una receta que tú sabes cocinar muy bien: _____

_____

5. Si a tu novio/a le encantan las rosas blancas: _____

6. Si tu amigo/a necesita usar tu computadora esta noche: _____

7. Si tus familiares quieren recibir un recuerdo (*souvenir*) de tu universidad: _____

_____

8. Si yo necesito un correo electrónico sobre tu experiencia sobre el estudio del español y este manual: _____

A: Si contestaste afirmativamente de 5 a 8 preguntas de este examen, eres una persona generosa.

B: Si contestaste afirmativamente sólo de 1 a 4 preguntas, ¡necesitas trabajar en este aspecto de tu personalidad!

4. *Gustar* and similar verbs

6-8   Tus opiniones. With a classmate write a list of things, people, and ideas that your other classmates may have an interest in or an opinion of. Then, ask some of your classmates about them. Make sure you use verbs like **gustar**, **interesar**, **importar**, **preocupar**, etc.

MODELO: PAREJA 1:   1. *La liga de fútbol europea*
                             2. *El calentamiento del planeta*
              PAREJA 1:   Pregunta: *¿Qué opinas/opinan sobre la liga de fútbol europea?*
              PAREJA 2:   E1: *No sé, no conozco mucho el fútbol, pero me gusta saber sobre los deportes.*

              PAREJA 1:   Pregunta: *¿Cuál es tu opinión sobre el calentamiento del planeta?*
              PAREJA 2:   E2: *A mí el calentamiento del planeta me preocupa mucho, creo que a todas las personas les interesan los problemas ambientales.*

Opiniones sobre . . .

1. _____

2. _____

3. _____

4. _____

5. _____

6. _____

7. _____

8. _____

9. _____

10. _____

Nombre: _____   Fecha: _____

5. More about *ser* and *estar*

6-9 ¿Cómo es la ropa? Think of three different occasions or events and what clothing y
would wear for each. Then write down a description of the outfit you would wear, includi
what material each item of clothing is made of. Read your descriptions to a partner and se
he or she can guess what each occasion or event is.

Ocasión #1

_____

_____

_____

Ocasión #2

_____

_____

_____

Ocasión #3

_____

_____

_____

6-10 Una boda espectacular. Read the following description of Anita and Raúl's wedding
Complete the sentences with the correct form of **ser** or **estar**.

¡Anita y Raúl se casan hoy! La boda (1) _____ en un lugar muy bonito en el centro
de Caracas. Todos los amigos y las familias de ellos (2) _____ allí. Anita
(3) _____ llevando un vestido color crema que (4) _____ precioso! El
vestido (5) _____ de seda y tiene unas perlas muy pequeñas y lindas que
(6) _____ en la parte de la falda. Ella (7) _____ muy bonita hoy—¡un día
tan importante! Raúl (8) _____ muy guapo en su etiqueta (*tuxedo*). La etiqueta
(9) _____ de seda y algodón y (10) _____ muy elegante. Todos los
invitados (11) _____ llevando ropa fina y elegante. ¡Los novios (12) _____
muy felices!

Nombre: _____   Fecha: _____ ■

MOSAICOS

6-11 Crucigrama. De compras. Ana is telling you what she did yesterday in the text below. Use the text to help you find the answers and then fill in the blank spaces with the following verbs in the preterit.

These are the infinitive forms: **comprar**, **ir**, **quedar**, **comer**, **barrer**, **encantar**, **probar**, **cambiar** (but not in this order!)

Now, decide which personal form in the preterit you need to find in your crossword puzzle in order to fill in the blank spaces below!

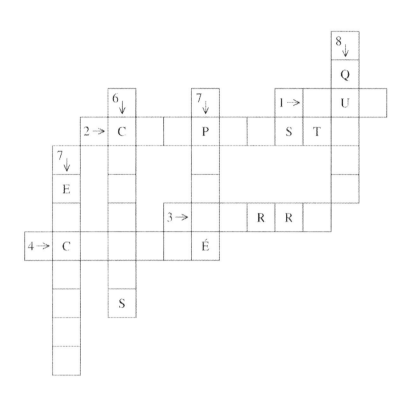

Ayer (1)_____de compras al nuevo centro comercial con Marina y Gustavo. Allí encontré el mismo impermeable azul que tú (2) _____ la semana pasada. Antes de salir de la casa, yo (3) _____ todo el piso de la casa y del patio. Por eso estaba (*I was*) muy cansada. En el centro comercial fui a la zapatería y (4) _____ los zapatos que mis padres me regalaron por mi cumpleaños porque eran (*were*) demasiado pequeños. Me (5) _____este nuevo centro comercial, es precioso y hay muchas tiendas de ropa. Marina, Gustavo y yo (6) _____ un bocadillo, y después en las boutiques me (7) _____muchas faldas pero no me gustó ninguna; sin embargo, este suéter de algodón me (8) _____ perfecto, por eso decidí comprarlo.

Capítulo 6 De compras ■ 87

6-12   Desfile de moda. You will design a fashion show for the yearly Convención de Nu
Moda Venezolana (New Venezuelan Fashion Convention) with your classmates. For this
activity you will need to bring some clothing, magazine clippings, or invent your own
designs with the clothes you and your classmates are wearing. You will form groups of th
or four. Each group will present one season's collection.

Choose from the following collections:

1. Verano

2. Otoño

3. Invierno

4. Primavera

5. Naturaleza y montaña

6. Celebraciones

7. Profesional

8. Moda joven

Paso 1. Each group will make a list of the clothing they think appropriate for their collecti
according to season and purpose. Each item must be listed along with its characteristics:
color, material, and occasion. Give a catchy name to your collection.

Colección # ____ : _____

MODELO	COLOR	MATERIAL	OCASIÓN

Paso 2. Each group will present its collection to the class. Use your imagination: Use pictures, clippings from magazines, and clothes you brought for this activity, or try to "create" fashionable clothing with the items you are wearing at the moment. There will be two "top models" and one presenter.

Paso 3. Each group will report about another group's collection for a fashion magazine. The report will begin as follows:

Informe sobre la Convención de Nueva Moda Venezolana

Ayer, en el Centro de Moda de la capital de Venezuela, se presentaron las colecciones de moda más audaces (daring) *para todas las temporadas.*

*La colección "*_____*", *_____

_____

_____

_____

_____

_____

_____

_____

_____

_____

_____

6-13 Entrevista con los famosos. With a group of students, think of a person who is famous because of the way he/she dresses and/or for his/her opinions on certain matters. You will interview this person and ask about: what he/she wears at different events or in different situations; his/her opinions on certain controversial topics; and his/her recommendations on some of the topics already discussed. The other students in the class will guess who this person is!

NOTE: Make sure that you use: 1) verbs of opinion, likes, and dislikes, such as **gustar, interesar, importar, caer bien,** etc.; 2) indirect object pronouns when necessary; 3) vocabulary related to clothes presented in the chapter; 4) if possible, the preterit tense.

Nombre: _____   Fecha: _____

Paso 1. First, write down the name of the person you will interview in your group and the questions you will ask.

Nombre: _____

Gustos, opiniones y preferencias:

_____

_____

_____

_____

_____

_____

_____

_____

Preguntas:

1. ¿ _____

2. ¿ _____

3. ¿ _____

4. ¿ _____

5. ¿ _____

6. ¿ _____

7. ¿ _____

8. ¿ _____

9. ¿ _____

10. ¿ _____

Paso 2. Now, perform your interview in front of the class. Your classmates will guess the name of this celebrity based on the answers.

ENFOQUE CULTURAL

6-14 Ecoturismo en el Parque Nacional Canaima. Using the preterit tense, you and your friend will write a review for a low-budget travel guide of a tour of the eastern region of Venezuela and the Parque Nacional Canaima based on your trip to this region last month. For your background knowledge, you will need to access the section on Venezuela on the *Mosaicos* webpage: http://www.prenhall.com/mosaicos, http://www.guiadelmundo.com, then click on Venezuela, or find information on the Parque Nacional Canaima using a search engine. Write a report of the places you saw and the activities you did, where you spent the night, the food you ate, and the types of clothing you needed for this adventure. Finally, give two recommendations to future travelers on important aspects of this trip.

Ecoturismo en Canaima: El paraíso de la aventura

7

Los deportes

A PRIMERA VISTA

7-1   Estrellas del deporte. A few students will perform as secret sports celebrities in front of the class. The rest of the class will divide into groups of three or four, and will think up five yes/no questions to ask these mystery stars about their sports. The questions will be about how the sport is played, during what season of the year and what the weather is like when this sport is played, how many players are needed, what equipment one needs to play it, etc.

MODELO: ¿Juegas este deporte con un balón? → *No, no lo juego con un balón.*

7-2   Los torneos. Think of a national or international sport event (**torneo**). In groups of three, write the name of the sport, where it is held, the season when it happens (give a full description of the season and weather conditions, temperatures included), and a description of the sport(s) played at this event: equipment needed, number of players, etc. Another group of students or the whole class should guess what the sport is.

FUNCIONES Y FORMAS

1. Preterit of reflexive verbs and pronouns

7-3   La rutina diaria. Paso 1. With a classmate make a list of your typical daily activities: wake up, shower, shave, brush your teeth, go to bed, etc.

Paso 2. Then, go around the classroom, asking students when they performed these activities this morning, yesterday, or last night, if at all. Have them sign their name in the chart below.

MODELO: *¿Te afeitaste esta mañana? ¿A qué hora te afeitaste?*

Encuesta

ACTIVIDAD	CUANDO	HORA DEL DÍA	FIRMA AQUÍ

2. Preterit of -*er* and -*ir* verbs whose stem ends in a vowel

7-4   ¡Una carrera! The class will divide into two teams. Each team will form a line in front of the board. The instructor will call out a verb and a subject and the person at the head of the line will go to the board and write the correct verb form in the preterit tense. The first person who writes the verb correctly will win a point for his or her team. The team with the most points at the end wins!

(Note: Use the following verbs in all forms to see if students remember to add the **y** to the third-person singular and plural preterit forms: **oír**, **leer**, **creer**, **construir**, **concluir**, and **contribuir**. You may also expand this activity by including preterit of reflexive verbs and pronouns, and preterit of stem-changing **-ir** verbs.)

3. Preterit of stem-changing -*ir* verbs

7-5   De boca en boca. In a group of five or six students, sit in a circle. One student will start an extraordinary story in the past tense by whispering it to the student next to him or her. Then, the second student will tell the third student the story; as the story is retold it will change slightly. The last student to hear the story will retell it to the group, and the changes that have occurred will be noted. Make sure you use the verbs presented in *Funciones y formas* on pages 238–239 of your textbook.

MODELO: E1: *¡Ayer llovieron sapos* (toads) *en el estado de Maine!*
                E2: *¡Oí que ayer llovieron sapos en el estado de Maine!*
                E3: *¡Mi amigo oyó que ayer llovieron sapos en el estado de Maine!*
                    Pero yo leí que ayer llovieron carros en el estado de Maine . . .
                E4: *Mi amigo leyó que ayer llovieron carros en el estado de Maine,*
                    pero yo leí que ayer regalaron carros en el estado de Maine . . .
                E5: *Mi amigo leyó que ayer regalaron carros en el estado de Maine,*
                    ¿Es verdad o es mentira?
                E1: *¡No es verdad! ¡Yo oí que ayer llovieron sapos, no que regalaron*
                    carros en el estado de Maine!

7-6   Noticias de actualidad. Think of an important event that happened recently: a political issue, a sports event, a celebration, etc.

Paso 1. You and your partner will write a brief account of this event, using the preterit tense.

Paso 2. Exchange your report with that of another pair, or report orally to other pairs. The other students will comment on the story: what you heard about this piece of news, what y read, and their opinions. Make sure you use verbs such as **oír**, **leer**, **preferir**, and **ver**.

MODELO: PAREJA 1: *Las Olimpiadas de Invierno:*
Las Olimpiadas de Invierno comenzaron el 2 de enero en Suiza.
El esquiador ganador del slalom fue un alemán...
ESTUDIANTES: *Yo oí que el ganador fue un suizo. / Yo leí que el ganador fue un argentino.*

4. Pronouns after prepositions

7-7 Despistados. You and your roommate are very absentminded and forget with whom you did things and why. Ask each other questions about what you did last week and whom you did things with.

Paso 1. Make a list of several activities you did last weekend. Make sure you write about them in full sentences with the verbs in the preterit.

Actividades:

_____

_____

_____

_____

_____

_____

_____

Paso 2. Exchange the list with your partner's and ask each other questions about what you did and how you did it. Make sure you find out details about your roommate's activities: people involved, reasons or purpose for doing them, etc. (Make sure you review *Emphasizin or clarifying information: Pronouns after prepositions* page 241 of your textbook, for this activity.)

MODELO: E1: *Fui a ver un partido de béisbol, y antes de esto, compré un regalo en el centr comercial.*
E2: *¿Con quién fuiste al partido? ¿Para quién compraste un regalo?*
E1: *¡Fui al partido contigo! ¿No lo recuerdas? Y compré un regalo para ti, también!*

Nombre: _____   Fecha: _____

5. Some irregular preterits

7-8 Reporteros del deporte. Paso 1. Find information about a sports game (baseball, soccer, basketball) that you enjoyed watching or reading about. With your classmate, write down a few notes on the highlights of the match.

Partido (*game*): _____

Equipos o jugadores: _____

Puntos para cada equipo: _____

Momentos importantes del partido: _____

_____

_____

Paso 2. With your partner, you will do a sports report for the whole class. Make sure you include the following verbs (among others) in the preterit in your oral report (see pages 243–244 of *Funciones y formas*, "Some irregular preterits").

querer	**saber**
poner	**venir**
poder	**hacer**
tener	

MOSAICOS

7-9 Ayer, hoy y mañana. You and your partner will give a weather report of a region of Spanish-speaking world. For this exercise you will need to access a weather website (for example, http://www.weatherchannel.com) and study the weather in the city or region that you choose. Alternatively, your teacher may assign you to do research on a specific city or region. First, you will need to describe the season: Is it winter? summer? spring? fall? Wh was the weather like yesterday? What is it like today and what will it be like tomorrow? Remember: In most countries temperatures are measured in the Celsius scale.

Make sure that you use preterit verbs (irregular-stem verbs such as **hacer**, **estar**, **tener** and other verbs will be necessary).

7-10 Deportes inusuales. With a classmate, find out about a sport you consider uncommo in the United States, such as jai-alai, or an adventure sport or one of the so called "extreme sports." Make sure that you find out how the sport is played, how many people are needed the equipment you need to play it, and the basic rules of the game.

Paso 1. Make a chart on the board, or on construction paper, with the number of players, th equipment needed to play the sport, and a set of basic rules. You can illustrate your presentation with pictures or clippings.

Paso 2. Present the sport to your classmates. Describe in detail the information presented o the board or on your poster. If you can, try to act it out.

Paso 3. Choose one of the sports presented by another pair, and write a fictional report of this sports event. Imagine that you attended a game or event where this sport was played. You will use the preterit in your narration. Also, give a brief account of the weather conditions during the sports event.

Deporte: _____

Mi amigo y yo fuimos a _____

_____

_____

_____

_____

_____

_____

_____

_____

_____

_____

_____

_____

_____. *¡Fue muy interesante y lo pasamos fenomenal!*

ENFOQUE CULTURAL

7-11 Mensaje secreto. Paso 1. You will find nine words hidden in the boxed text. Move from left to right. With the result, you will be able to compose the name of a famous athle~~te~~ and the sport he or she plays. First, write down the words you find with the help of clues ~~1~~ below. Second, write the letters called for in the spaces provided. From top to bottom, you will be able to read the player's name and the sport.

A	Q	B	A	R	B	A	R	O	T	L	E	V	A	N
T	A	R	S	E	N	M	M	D	R	T	S	O	L	K
M	O	F	E	D	O	R	M	I	R	M	K	J	G	W
F	L	O	R	E	S	U	R	U	G	U	A	Y	O	Q
B	T	I	N	P	B	A	L	O	N	K	P	A	L	O

Pistas:

1. Significa "fenomenal" en el español de Uruguay:

    _____   tercera letra → _____

    séptima letra → _____

2. Es lo primero que haces todas las mañanas:

    _____   quinta letra → _____

    séptima letra → _____

3. En verano siempre hace . . .

    _____   tercera letra → _____

4. Cuando te acuestas, te vas a . . .

    _____   primera letra → _____

    segunda Letra → _____

5. En la primavera y el verano hay muchas:

    _____   primera letra → _____

6. Su capital es Montevideo:

_____   quinta letra →   _____

7. Pronombre:

_____   primera letra →   _____

8. Se juega a baloncesto con él:

_____   primera letra →   _____

                                     cuarta letra →   _____

9. Se juega al golf con él:

_____   tercera letra →   _____

Paso 2. Find information about this player. Write a paragraph with a classmate in which you relate this sportsman's main achievements. Where is he from? Where did he start to play? What were his most important achievements in the past years/months? Where is he now and for what team does he play?

```
_____

_____

_____

_____

_____

_____

_____

_____

_____

_____
```

7-12 Argentina and Uruguay. Find information on popular sports in Argentina and Uruguay. With a classmate, write a description of the sport, its teams or players, and famo sport stars from this country. Give a brief report to your classmates on your findings.

_____
_____
_____
_____
_____
_____
_____
_____
_____
_____

7-13 Dos atletas argentinos. Find information on Leonel Messi and Manu Ginobili, who are both well known professional athletes from Argentina. Write a brief paragraph on each player in which you indicate what sports they play, for which teams, where, etc. Give a brie report to your classmates on your findings.

_____
_____
_____
_____
_____
_____
_____
_____
_____
_____

CAPÍTULO

8

Nuestras tradiciones

A PRIMERA VISTA

8-1 La fecha secreta. Think of an important date for your country, region, town, or university. Alternatively, research some important Hispanic celebrations. One or two classmates will try to guess the holiday or important date by asking you questions about it. Make sure your answers give details on activities, foods, etc., during this celebration.

8-2 ¡Nos casamos! Think of a famous couple and design a wedding plan for them.

Paso 1. With a classmate, make a plan for the wedding: place, date and time, type of ceremony, festivities or celebrations involved, transportation, guests, etc. You may use the information in *Otras celebraciones* on pages 260–261 of your textbook.

Plan de boda

Novios: _____

Lugar, fecha y hora: _____

Padres del novio: _____

Padres de la novia: _____

Invitados principales: _____

Tipo de ceremonia: _____

Celebración: _____

Otras actividades: _____

Paso 2. Now, call some of the guests (another pair) and ask them if they received their invitation and if they are planning to attend the wedding. The guests will ask you question pertinent to the wedding, the date and place, and dress code. They will either accept or decline the invitation. Then exchange roles. Make sure you review the information present in *Otras celebraciones* on pages 260–261 of your textbook.

8-3   La música. In some Spanish-speaking countries music is an important component of celebrations and holidays. Mariachi music from Mexico (see the *Cultura* box on page 263 an example of a type of music popular at celebrations. The Tunas are university musical groups from Spain, and Punta music from Honduras is another popular musical genre.

Paso 1. Divide into several groups. Find information about these musical organizations, an others that you know or have heard of, their activities, the type of celebrations where they entertain, the instruments and type of music they play, etc. For information on this topic go http://www.geocities.com/kaibigankastil/tuna.html,
http://www.explorandomexico.com.mx/about-mexico/5/127/,
http://www.stanford.edu/group/arts/honduras/discovery_sp/art/dance/punta2.html, and
http://www.flamefilms.com/spirit/musica.htm, or find information by doing your own Internet search on Mariachi(s), Tuna(s), and Punta music.

Paso 2. Present the information as if you belonged to one of these musical groups. You can bring pictures and objects to personify the important aspects of these groups and, if your classroom has multimedia, show a video clip or play a song.

FUNCIONES Y FORMAS

1. The imperfect

8-4 Infancia Real. Imagine that you have the chance to interview Prince Felipe of Spain and his wife, Doña Letizia Ortiz. For information on this royal couple go to http://www.casareal.es or to *A primera vista, Celebraciones personales* on page 263 of your textbook. In groups of three, prepare an interview of the couple about what life was like before they got married. Obviously, their childhood was very different! Ask them questions about their studies, their pastimes, their schooling, and other habitual actions of their childhood, adolescence, and youth.

Paso 1. Before you start the interview, make sure you have enough basic information on the couple: date and place of birth, where they studied, their professional activities, their family members, etc.

FELIPE   **LETIZIA**

_____   _____

_____   _____

_____   _____

_____   _____

_____   _____

_____   _____

_____   _____

_____   _____

_____   _____

Paso 2. Now, perform the interview in front of the class or a group of students. Each one of you will take a role: Prince Felipe, Princess Letizia, and host. Make sure you use the imperfect tense when appropriate.

8-5 Los viejos tiempos. Call up or write to an older member of your family: your grandparent, an aunt or uncle, or your parents. Think of a particular object, activity, or top that you consider a relevant part of your life and theirs, for example, television, movies, telephone, public transportation, college, etc. What is it like now, and what was it like in t youth? Ask them questions about it. Then report to a group of students or the class on thei answers. Make sure you use the imperfect tense to do your oral report.

Familiar: _____

Objeto/actividad/tema: _____

Cómo era antes: _____

_____

_____

_____

_____

_____

_____

2. The preterit and the imperfect

8-6 Un momento inolvidable. Bring a personal snapshot to class. Make sure this picture captures an interesting point in time that you recall well: an important or special event such as a trip, a reunion, a celebration, a sports event, etc.

Paso 1. A. Look at the picture and decide what the story behind the picture is. Write down what happened before, during, and after the picture was taken.

B. Decide what aspects are descriptive about this moment: the weather, the people who were there, the circumstances, etc.

Now write these ideas in two columns, La historia and Las circunstancias.

LA HISTORIA	LAS CIRCUNSTANCIAS

Paso 2. Share your picture with a group of students. Relate to them the information you wrote in the chart. Make sure you use complete sentences and the preterit and imperfect tenses as appropriate, depending on whether you are telling about the events that took place (the story) or the circumstances (description, evaluation, commentaries) of the story.

3. Comparisons of inequality

8-7   Celebraciones. Call your parents or a family member and ask them about important celebrations in your family. Ask them what has changed in the way they used to celebrate them during their childhood and adolescence, and now.

Paso 1. With a classmate compare your notes. Make a list of the celebrations and the differences family members pointed out.

CELEBRACIÓN	ANTES	AHORA

Paso 2. Write a report in which you compare these celebrations before and now. Were they more or less fun? Were the celebrations longer or shorter? Was there more or less food/music/singing? Were there more or fewer people involved? How are the celebrations different?

4. Comparisons of equality

8-8 Diego Rivera and Frida Kahlo: Two famous Mexican painters. Find a painting by one of them and your partner will find a painting by the other. Bring a reproduction to class (a postcard, a printout, a book).

Paso 1. First, write down the most distinctive features you see in this painting.

Pintura y artista: _____

Características: _____

_____

_____

_____

Paso 2. With your classmate, examine your two paintings and notes, and draw some comparisons that speak of the colors, texture, style, the artistic movement the artists belonged to, etc. Write a report based on your comparisons.

5. The superlative

8-9 Los -*ísimos*. With a classmate make a list of celebrations you consider typical of you family, university, region, etc.

Paso 1. Decide whether these celebrations are interesting, funny, boring, important, etc. Write the adjective that in your opinion describes them best, according to your discussion. Then, move around the classroom asking your classmates what they think of these celebrations: Do they agree or disagree with you? Would they describe these celebrations with a different adjective? Mark down their opinions in the two boxes provided below **(de acuerdo / en desacuerdo).**

CELEBRACIÓN	DESCRIPCIÓN	DE ACUERDO	EN DESACUERD

Paso 2. Check the number of responses and then report on these, using the superlative. Elaborate as much as possible on your answers, presenting your classmates' preferences as well as yours.

MODELO: 4 de julio → divertida   de acuerdo → 5 estudiantes
                                          en desacuerdo → importante —10 estudiantes
          *La mayoría de nuestros compañeros piensan que el 4 de julio es una fiesta
          importantísima. Aunque nosotros pensamos que no es la más importante, creemo
          que es divertidísima.*

MOSAICOS

8-10 SOPA DE LETRAS. Paso 1. Find the words in this puzzle that complete the statements below. Review the vocabulary list on page 289 of your textbook to complete this exercise.

C	A	R	R	E	T	A	R	I	G	P	J
E	A	H	M	N	K	E	B	F	H	P	F
M	A	R	I	A	C	H	I	S	R	R	Q
E	W	I	N	V	I	T	A	C	I	O	N
N	Q	Z	X	A	V	B	W	O	J	C	D
T	R	A	V	C	V	W	Y	M	P	E	N
E	R	L	Z	B	R	A	H	P	K	S	O
R	Q	K	T	P	G	P	L	A	Y	I	K
I	D	F	J	S	B	T	W	R	U	O	L
O	R	Q	U	E	S	T	A	S	D	N	Q
Z	H	G	Y	W	U	Y	T	A	M	W	K

1. Es una celebración muy famosa en Oruro, Bolivia: _____

2. Se utiliza en la Peregrinación del Rocío, en España, para transportar a las personas: _____

3. Son cantantes y músicos que animan celebraciones acompañados de guitarras: _____

4. La gente ve pasar este desfile religioso durante la Semana Santa: _____

5. En este evento, un hombre se enfrenta a un toro en una plaza: _____

6. La necesitas para poder asistir a una boda: _____

7. En muchas bodas, un grupo de música y
   canto en vivo que toca para que la gente baile: _____

8. El Día de los Muertos, la gente de México va a
   este lugar para visitar a sus familiares muertos: _____

Paso 2. Choosing four terms that relate to the traditions of a country or a geographical reg
of the Spanish-speaking world, write a letter to a friend in which you relate your cultural
experience in the country or countries: where you went, what you saw, and what you
experienced in these celebrations. Using the preterit and the imperfect tenses, narrate your
travels, compare the experiences, and tell your friend which one was the best of all and wh

Una experiencia increíble

_____

_____

_____

_____

_____

_____

_____

_____

_____

_____

_____

8-11 La vida del inmigrante. With a group of students, find a person (a neighbor, an international student, an employee at the university, etc.) from another country. Ideally, this person should be of Hispanic origin, but you may interview a person from any other country. With your classmates, design an interview in which you ask this person about celebrations, activities, and customs that he/she used to engage in before moving to the United States. Ask him/her what is different now in his or her life, the types of celebrations, activities, etc.

Paso 1. Make a list of possible questions to ask this person.

1. ¿_____?
2. ¿_____?
3. ¿_____?
4. ¿_____?
5. ¿_____?
6. ¿_____?
7. ¿_____?
8. ¿_____?

Paso 2. After your interview, give an account of the information you gathered. Write a report with your classmates that includes who this person is, how his/her life was before immigrating, the differences between past and present life, the cultural differences and affinities (e.g., differences between U.S. festivities and those of his/her country of origin), etc.

_____

_____

_____

_____

_____

_____

_____

_____

_____

_____

ENFOQUE CULTURAL

8-12 A cada país su celebración. The class will be divided into groups of three or four students. Each group will be responsible for researching cultural information on Mexico a͏͏ two other Spanish-speaking countries of their choice. You can start your research by reviewing the information presented in *Enfoque cultural* on pages 286–287 of your textbo͏ also, visit http://www.guiadelmundo.com and other pertinent websites.

Each group will research one category from those listed below.

A: fiesta religiosa de invierno
B: fiesta religiosa de primavera o verano
C: fiesta laica (no religiosa)
D: fiesta única de este país (*a unique celebration of this country*)
E: culturas indígenas de estos países (*native culture(s) in these countries*)
F: yacimientos arqueológicos en estos países (*archaeological sites of this country*)

NOTE: If one of the other countries is Spain, note that the term "indigenous" does not app͏ Replace "indigenous" with "minority" in E.

Paso 1. First, list the event or topic you are researching and then your findings for each country.

Grupo: _____   Tema: _____

México:

_____

_____

_____

Otro:

_____

_____

_____

Otro:

_____

_____

_____

Paso 2. Now, present your findings orally to the class. Make sure you draw comparisons (equality, inequality, and superlative) among the three countries. You may present visual aids such as an outline of the major points, or, if possible, pictures that illustrate your points.

....
CAPÍTULO

9

Hay que trabajar

A PRIMERA VISTA

9-1 Lugares y profesiones. Bring a number of magazine photos to class showing different locations: a construction site, a strip mall, a bank, etc.

Paso 1. With a classmate, list all the different jobs related to each location. You'll be amazed at how many people are needed to run any of these places!

MODELO: lugar: un banco   profesiones: ejecutivo/a
                                 secretario/a
                                 contable o contador/a
                                 mensajero/a (*courier*)
                                 economista
                                 señor/a de la limpieza
                                 guarda de seguridad

LUGAR   **PROFESIONES**

1. _____   _____

                                    _____

                                    _____

2. _____   _____

                                    _____

                                    _____

3. _____   _____

                                    _____

                                    _____

Paso 2. Give a brief description of one of these professions and its main responsibilities.

_____

_____

_____

_____

_____

_____

_____

_____

_____

_____

9-2 Bolsa de trabajo. In class you will create a job fair for your school. Half of the class (Grupo A) will offer jobs to the students, and the other half (Grupo B) will be looking for a job.

Paso 1.

Grupo A: Think of jobs that college students typically hold during their college years or right after graduation. In groups of two or three students, create two job ads. Give the job title, a brief description of responsibilities, and the required qualifications for the job. Be creative and original. You can make up new professions. Follow some of the ads presented throughout this chapter in your textbook, or if you have the chance, look up different job ads written in Spanish in Spanish newspapers or on the Internet.

Grupo B: In pairs or groups of three students, each of you will develop your professional profile. Make a list of your work experience, your qualifications, and your potential or goals. Then, walk around the classroom and find a job that suits your profile.

Paso 2. Teams of Grupo A will create different booths in class with their job offers. Students of Grupo B will walk around the room looking for the ideal job according to their professional profile. If they think they are suitable for a job, they will express their interest and present their qualifications to the employers. The employers will ask them questions.

Paso 3. Each team of Grupo A will present their best job applicant. They will say why they think he or she is the best candidate for the job they offer.

FUNCIONES Y FORMAS

1. Review of direct and indirect object pronouns

9-3   Prueba de generosidad. Once again, let's test your generosity. Give answers to the following questions using direct and indirect pronouns. Then, check your answers and find out how generous you were to others. Compare your answers with those of your classmate, and write a report about your classmate's acts of generosity.

Say whether you have ever done the following things for others.

MODELO: ¿Alguna vez . . . le prestaste tu tarjeta de crédito a un amigo/a?
A: *Sí, le presté mi tarjeta de crédito a un amigo/a.*
B: *¡No, no le presté mi tarjeta de crédito a un amigo/a.*

Note: Make sure you use a variety of verbs: **dar, entregar, prestar, enviar, hacer, llevar,** etc.

¿Alguna vez . . .

1. le prestaste el coche a un amigo/a?

2. le ayudaste a cruzar la calle a una persona mayor?

3. le hiciste una fiesta de cumpleaños a un familiar?

4. le pintaste la casa a tu madre?

5. le compraste flores a tu novio/a?

6. les escribiste cartas de solicitud de trabajo a tus amigos/as?

7. les enviaste un recuerdo (*souvenir*) de tu universidad a tus abuelos?

8. nos enviaste tus sugerencias para escribir una nueva edición de este manual?

9. unos ladrones (*thieves*) te robaron el dinero y tú les diste también tu abrigo?

10. alguien te dijo que eres una persona super-generosa?

Nombre: _____   Fecha: _____

Clave:

A: Si contestaste afirmativamente de 7 a 10 preguntas de esta prueba, eres una persona mu
generosa. Lo haces todo por otros. Todos te quieren y te están muy agradecidos.

B: Si contestaste afirmativamente de 4 a 6 preguntas, eres generoso/a pero necesitas segui
trabajando en este aspecto de tu personalidad. Aunque puedes hacerlo mejor, las personas
estiman la ayuda que les puedes dar.

C: Si has contestado afirmativamente sólo de 1 a 3 preguntas, no eres una persona generos
en absoluto. Tu vida va a ser mejor si logras mejorar este aspecto de tu personalidad.

2. Use of direct and indirect object pronouns together

9-4. La generosidad. Share your answers with a classmate but, before you do, rewrite yo
answers using the direct and indirect object pronouns together.

MODELO: ¿Alguna vez . . . le prestaste tu tarjeta de crédito a un amigo/a?
    A: *Sí, se la presté.*
    B: *¡No, no se la presté.*

9-5 ¡Somos generosos! In order to show others that you and your friend are really genero
people, come up with three things you consider great acts of generosity.

MODELO: *Cuando veo a una señora con muchas bolsas, ¡yo se las llevo / nosotros(as) se
    llevamos!*

1. _____

2. _____

3. _____

Nombre: _____   Fecha: _____

9-6 En la comisaría. Unfortunately, on your spring-break trip you and your friends were victims of a robbery. You need to report it to the police station. Create a dialog in which you report the theft to a police officer, who will ask you questions about the unfortunate event. Make sure you use direct and indirect object pronouns together.

MODELO: Policía: *¿Les robaron las tarjetas de crédito?*
Víctima: *Sí, a mi amigo se las robaron, pero a mí no.*

EN LA COMISARÍA

POLICÍA: _____

VÍCTIMA: _____

POLICÍA: _____

VÍCTIMA: _____

POLICÍA: _____

VÍCTIMA: _____

POLICÍA: _____

VÍCTIMA: _____

POLICÍA: _____

VÍCTIMA: _____

3. More on the imperfect and preterit

9-7 Lo supe. Think of an opportunity you had in life that allowed you to do something th[at] you consider life-changing or extremely important. Recall that time, giving details of wha[t] was happening at the time the event occurred, and your actions and choices. Make sure yo[u] use the imperfect progressive to describe the situation and verbs such as **conocer**, **querer**, **poder**, and **saber**, understanding the different meanings these verbs convey when used in preterit and the imperfect.

_____

_____

_____

_____

_____

_____

_____

_____

_____

_____

9-8 Una escena del pasado. Bring some magazine pictures of people engaged in work an[d] professional situations. They can be politicians or professionals pictured in news magazine[s] or people in advertisements. With a classmate, decide what was happening when this pictur[e] was taken. Create a story around the scene: Who was doing what? What was being discussed? Why did certain things look a certain way? Give logical explanations for the events depicted in the scene.

4. Formal commands

9-9 Una emergencia. You are a professor's research assistant. Your professor had a medical emergency and will be in the hospital for three weeks. He or she calls you and asks you to take care of the office, the research projects, the students who stop by to ask for help, and other important chores.

Paso 1. Make a list of the things your professor may need you to do during this time away.

TAREAS	FRECUENCIA

Paso 2. With a classmate, create a dialog in which you ask your professor about these tasks and when you are supposed to perform them. Your professor will answer, giving you commands. Make sure you use direct and indirect object pronouns in your questions and answers.

MODELO: leer el correo electrónico   cada día
       E1: *¿Le debo leer el correo electrónico?/¿Le leo el correo electrónico?*
       E2: *Sí, por favor, léemelo.*
       E1: *¿Cuándo debo leerlo?*
       E2: *Léemelo cada día.*

9-10 Consejos profesionales. You and your friend work at a job placement agency givin[g] professional advice on how to behave in a job interview, what to write in a cover letter, w[hat] to include in a résumé, etc. You want to be clear and direct with your clients; for this reas[on] you will advise them with direct commands.

Paso 1. With your partner, create a list of jobs for which to provide advice, as well as a lis[t of] things people should do or should not do when applying or interviewing for these jobs.

TRABAJO	QUÉ HACER/QUÉ NO HACER

Paso 2. Exchange lists with another pair. You will inquire about what to do or not to do based on the list you receive.

MODELO: Modelo masculine   Vestirse de forma apropiada (*proper*)
>   E1: *Tengo una entrevista para ser modelo masculino en una revista de ropa juvenil. ¿Debo llevar traje?*
>   E2: *¡No! lleve ropa de una tienda juvenil! / No, vístase con una camiseta negra y* [*pantalones de cuero.*
>   E1: *¿Debo pedirle ayuda a mi madre para comprar ese tipo de ropa?*
>   E2: *No, ¡pídasela a su novia!*

MOSAICOS

9-11 Ensalada de palabras. Paso 1. The following string of letters contains seven verbs related to job hunting. Find the seven verbs, and then give advice to a potential job seeker on what to do when applying for a job. Review the vocabulary list on page 325 of your textbook to complete this exercise.

G	R	R	K	E	N	V	I	A	R	M	L	O	P	L	L	E	N	A	R
G	M	J	H	O	C	O	M	U	N	I	C	A	R	L	K	O	N	Y	W
E	S	P	E	R	A	R	F	Z	X	S	O	L	I	C	I	T	A	R	D
A	P	A	G	A	R	J	O	I	B	Y	U	I	N	D	I	C	A	R	G

Respuestas: _____   _____   _____

_____   _____   _____   _____

Paso 2. Now, give advice to a potential job candidate. Complete the following commands with the appropriate verbs.

¡Ojo! One verb will not fit in any of the blanks!

1. _____ hasta encontrar un anuncio de trabajo apropiado a su perfil profesional.

2. _____ el puesto de trabajo con tiempo, antes de la fecha límite indicada en el anuncio.

3. _____ todos los formularios necesarios para solicitar este trabajo.

4. _____ su CV (*résumé*) con una carta de solicitud a la empresa.

5. En su carta, _____ sus puntos fuertes (*strengths*) al director de recursos humanos de la empresa de manera directa y optimista.

6. _____ sus datos personales en la carta: su número de teléfono y su dirección de correo electrónico.

ENFOQUE CULTURAL

9-12 Los trabajos de antes. In Capítulo 9 you learned about the history of the indigenous people of Guatemala and the industriousness with which they built their civilization. This industriousness continues today in many facets of modern life in Guatemala. In the puzzle below you will find thirteen words relating to various themes related to the Guatemalan industry, past and present. With a partner, find the words and write them in the appropriate column. The first two letters of each word have been included.

```
P  I  N  T  O  R  C  T  X  L  A  G  R  I  C  U  L  T  O  R  T  O  C  A  F  É

X  U  V  R  B  U  F  É  E  S  C  U  L  T  O  R  O  P  I  T  F  R  U  T  A  L

O  P  U  C  O  R  T  A  D  O  R  D  E  P  I  E  D  R  A  L  N  Í  Q  U  E  L

E  L  O  P  U  R  A  S  T  R  Ó  N  O  M  O  E  X  C  E  L  U  R  T  S  O

M  A  D  E  R  A  Z  E  T  I  L  C  A  R  P  I  N  T  E  R  O  T  I  F  A  Y

M  E  R  C  A  D  O  L  I  R  O  T  U  C  E  R  Á  M  I  C  A  K  E  P  F  O

I  S  P  T  E  C  A  Ñ  A  D  E  A  Z  Ú  C  A  R  C  A  R  T  I  M  S  E  R

C  O  P  R  P  L  Á  T  A  N  O  I  V  A  P  T  X  O  C  U  L  T  I  V  A  R
```

AGRICULTURE & NATURE	ARTS, CRAFTS & MANUAL LABOR	MINING & COMMERC
1. AS…_____	6. PL…_____	11. CA…_____
2. AG…_____	7. MA…_____	12. ME…_____
3. CU…_____	8. ES…_____	13. NÍ…_____
4. CA…_____	9. PI…_____	
5. CA…_____	10. CO…_____	

9-13 Buscar empleo en Guatemala. Paso 1. You will be graduating from college in several months and plan to fulfill your dream of moving to a Spanish-speaking country. Some of your friends who have traveled around Central America have told you that Guatemala is beautiful, so you have decided to look for a job there. Lucky thing you majored in Spanish! Using one of the following websites, select three jobs that interest you and write down the job titles, responsibilities, salaries, and locations, etc.

http://www.gt.computrabajo.com/bt-ofertas.htm

http://www.deguate.com/empleos/anuncios.shtml

TRABAJO	RESPONSABILIDADES	SALARIO	LUGAR
_____	_____	_____	_____
_____	_____	_____	_____
_____	_____	_____	_____

Paso 2. With a classmate, compare your lists. Tell your classmate which job he or she should apply for and why, and also what he or she should do to prepare. Use formal commands.

MODELO: E1: *Solicite el trabajo de contable en la ciudad de Guatemala porque tiene buen salario.*
E2: *Qué debo hacer?*
E1: *Escriba un correo electrónico a la empresa y dígales que estás interesado/a en el puesto. También, envíe tu currículum vitae.*

CAPÍTULO

10

¡A comer!

A PRIMERA VISTA

10-1 Un mercado ecuatoriano. For this activity, you will gather art and photos of fruits and vegetables. The class will be divided into pairs and two groups: A: Sellers and B: Buyers, for a farmers' market in Ecuador.

Paso 1.

Grupo A: The sellers will set up stands with the pictures of the foods and the prices for them. Each stand should have a variety of foods.

Grupo B: The buyers will have a set amount of money to buy the foods at the market. They need to negotiate prices with sellers and acquire as many items as possible.

Note: In most Hispanic countries, the weight unit is the kilo.

Paso 2. Each pair from Grupo B will report to the whole class on their purchases: what they bought and how much they spent on each item, as well as how much money is left after the purchases.

10-2 La nueva cocina. You and your classmate are taking cooking classes during your study-abroad experience in Ecuador. Your professor asks you to create a new, experiment menu with traditional ingredients. You must create two recipes based on typical Ecuadori dishes and write them down for the course cookbook you will publish at the end of the semester.

Paso 1. Do some basic research on typical South American vegetables, fruits, and meats, a well as on traditional recipes that are used in Ecuador. Then, list two traditional dishes and their ingredients.

Plato #1: _____ Ingredientes: _____

Plato #2: _____ Ingredientes: _____

Paso 2. Write down your two special recipes and present them to the whole class.

10-3 Receta familiar. Does your family have a special recipe that has been passed on from generation to generation? Contact a family member (your mom, your grandparent, your uncle, your aunt, etc.) and ask him/her for this recipe: its name, the ingredients and where to buy them, how to make it, and its approximate cost. Write the recipe here and do an oral report for your classmates in which you describe the dish and why it is special to your family.

Receta familiar:

_____

_____

_____

_____

_____

10-4 Protocolo de mesa. Your friend is setting the table for the following celebrations and events. He or she will ask you what food goes on the table. Make sure you give details about the prepared dishes, the utensils, the linens, the number of plates and glasses, and the condiments accompanying the meals.

1. Una cena del Día de Acción de Gracias

2. Un picnic con barbacoa

3. Una fiesta de cumpleaños

4. Un almuerzo informal en la casa

5. Una cena de sushi y comida asiática

6. Una merienda con los amigos

FUNCIONES Y FORMAS

1. *Se* + verb constructions

10-5 Carteles. You are responsible for a group of young people in the cafeteria of their school and decide to create signs with rules appropriate behavior and manners at the table. What are the things that should be done or not be done in at the table? Create signs using the *se* + verb construction. Then, hang all your signs on the walls and decide which ones are the most original. As you look at them, make sure you comment on the topic, the grammatical correctness, and the originality. Choose the three best signs.

2. Present perfect and participles used as adjectives

10-6 Experiencias culinarias. With your classmate, list some foods and meals that you have eaten, prepared, or bought that you consider unique, challenging, or special. Then, go around the classroom and ask your classmates about their culinary experiences. Do you have anything in common? What interesting things have they eaten, cooked, or bought? Did they like them?

MODELO: Comer ceviche →
    E1 y E2: *¿Has/han comido ceviche?*
    E3 y E4: *Yo sí he comido ceviche/nosotros sí hemos comido ceviche.*
    E1 y E2: *¡Firma aquí!/¡Firmen aquí!*
    → *Pablo y Susana han comido ceviche. Nosotros también lo hemos comido.*

COMIDA	QUIÉN	LE(S) GUSTÓ/NO LE(S) GUSTÓ

Nombre: _____   Fecha: _____

10-7 Dietas especiales. With a classmate, think of several situations in which you or someone you know has enjoyed or avoided certain foods and why. Verbs to use are **comer, evitar, comprar, preparar, gustar.**

Paso 1. Make a list below of the people, the foods, and the reasons.

PERSONAS	COMIDAS	RAZÓN

Paso 2. Get together with a group of students and take turns discussing the information you have written down.

MODELO: E1: *Mi padre*
            No ha comido la comida china porque tiene mucha sal.

3. Informal commands

10-8 Una receta favorita. Your roommate and you have decided to make your favorite dessert recipes. Think of what dessert is your favorite and write down the steps necessary to prepare it, from what to buy to how to make it. Then share the steps with your roommate and tell him or her what to do. Use informal commands.

Receta favorita

Pasos a seguir:

1. _____

2. _____

3. _____

4. _____

5. _____

etc. . . .

Nombre: _____   Fecha: _____

4. The future tense

10-9 Una fiesta de graduación. You and your friends are about to graduate from college and your families are planning a huge party to celebrate. Everyone will have to pitch in to make the celebration a success. Write down what each person in your family, and you and your friends, will do to plan this party.

MODELO: Yo → comprar las bebidas
Compraré los refrescos y las cervezas
La abuela de José → hacer un plato típico de su país
La abuela de José hará un plato típico de su país: el arroz con pollo.

Get together with a classmate to tell each other about the graduation parties you will have. Who will have the best party?

MOSAICOS

10-10 Comida étnica. With a classmate think of an ethnic restaurant in your town (Hispanic or other) that you both enjoy a lot.

Paso 1. Have a brainstorming session on the quality of the dishes and their condiments, the signature dishes or their ingredients in this restaurant, and the reasons why you think it is worth eating there.

RESTAURANTE	PLATOS	INGREDIENTES

Paso 2. Write a brief report for a local or student newspaper about this restaurant, presenting one or two of its signature dishes: a description, the list of ingredients, the taste, and the price.

_____

_____   _____
_____   _____
_____   _____
_____   _____
_____   _____
_____   _____
_____   _____
_____   _____

Paso 3. The whole class will discuss which restaurant they recommend and why.

ENFOQUE CULTURAL

10-11 Un mercado tradicional. Is there a traditional market in your town? Is there a farmers' market? If so, write a description of the market, the foods and other items that can be purchased in this market, the prices, and then compare it to a modern supermarket. Recommend what to buy, where, and why, or tell what you have bought there in the past.

_____

_____
_____
_____
_____
_____
_____
_____
_____
_____
_____
_____
_____
_____
_____

10-12 Cocina típica. The class will be divided into three groups (A, B, and C), and then in pairs. Each group will research one of the following traditional dishes of Ecuador:

Spring Soup (Fanesca)

Potato Cakes (Llapingachos)

Steamed Puddings (Quimbolitos)

Potato Soup (Locro)

Pumpkin Cake (Torta de Zapallo)

Paso 1. Each pair will do some research on their assigned dish. Within each group, all the pairs together will make a list in the chart below, or on the board, of the ingredients necessary to make their dish.

PLATO	INGREDIENTES

Paso 2. Each group will describe the dish assigned, the ingredients needed, and how to cook this dish. Make sure you use an impersonal form such as **se** + verb or formal commands to tell others how to create this dish.

CAPÍTULO

11

La salud es lo primero

Nombre: _____

Fecha: _____

A PRIMERA VISTA

11-1 La canción del verano. Create a "catchy" song with other students in the class following the model presented below. You will need to use the formal commands and words for the parts of the body.

MODELO: *Ésta es la canción del verano,*
Cántela conmigo, hermano:
Ahora, mueva la cadera, un, dos, tres
Ahora, dé un paso hacia atrás, un, dos, tres
Ahora, ponga el pie en la silla, un, dos, tres . . .
¡Ya está! ¿Empezamos otra vez?

Continue with the song, adding directions for other parts of the body. Put music or a rhythm to it, add lyrics, and act it out as you sing!

Ésta es la canción del verano,
Cántela conmigo, hermano:
Ahora un, dos, tres
Ahora un, dos, tres
Ahora un, dos, tres . . .
¡Ya está! ¿Empezamos otra vez?
Ésta es la canción del verano,
Cántela conmigo, hermano:
Ahora un, dos, tres
Ahora un, dos, tres
Ahora un, dos, tres . . .
¡Ya está! ¿Empezamos otra vez?

11-2 Los medicamentos. Think of two or three over-the-counter medicines.

Paso 1. Write down the kinds of symptoms these medicines address.

MEDICINA	SÍNTOMAS

Paso 2. Now, tell a classmate about a recent ailment: your symptoms, what you did to alleviate the pain or the illness, whether you saw a doctor, what the doctor prescribed or recommended.

11-3 Síntomas. What are the typical symptoms of the following ailments?

Paso 1. With a classmate, list the symptoms you know of these illnesses and medical problems. Note that in Spanish, the ending **-itis** is the common way to refer to "inflammation"; other technical terms such as "lumbago" are commonly used as well.

1. intoxicación por alimentos en mal estado

_____

_____

2. apendicitis

_____

_____

3. bronquitis

_____

_____

4. lumbago (dolor de espalda lumbar)

_____

_____

5. infección de oídos (otitis)

_____

_____

6. conjuntivitis (*pink eye*)

_____

_____

Paso 2. What should you do if you have any of these conditions? Give recommendations to a classmate for treatment for these problems. Then, exchange roles.

FUNCIONES Y FORMAS

1. Introduction to the present subjunctive

11-4 Remedios caseros. Paso 1. Did you ever—or do you still—use home remedies whe_ you were sick? Think about when you were little: did your parents or your grandparents e_ have you drink tea with honey or gargle with saltwater when you had a sore throat? Make list of some illnesses and ailments you have had and the home remedies—or remedies tha_ not involve prescribed or over-the counter medications.

ENFERMEDAD	REMEDIO CASERO
_____	_____
_____	_____
_____	_____
_____	_____
_____	_____

Paso 2. Get together with a classmate and read each other's lists. Then play the part of you_ classmate's mother or father, grandmother or grandfather, and tell him or her what home remedy you want him/her to take—or what to do. Use the following verbs: **querer**, **desear**_ **recomendar**, **insistir en**, etc.

MODELO: E1: *Si tienes un dolor de garganta, quiero que tomes té caliente con miel.*

2. The subjunctive with expressions of emotion

11-5 ¿Enfermos o no? You and a classmate are volunteers at an assisted-living center in your town. You listen to a lot of complaints from the elderly residents at the center. You are compassionate and you give advice to the elderly; however, your classmate is not so compassionate and expresses doubts about the real nature of these people's complaints.

Paso 1. In groups of three, make a list of typical health problems related to the elderly, as well as symptoms they may present.

PROBLEMA	SÍNTOMA

Paso 2. Create a dialog in which an elderly person complains about his or her health problems. One student will show sympathy and the other will express doubt and disbelief about the illnesses.

VIEJITO/A: _____

VOLUNTARIO 1: _____

VOLUNTARIO 2: _____

VIEJITO/A: _____

VOLUNTARIO 1: _____

VOLUNTARIO 2: _____

VIEJITO/A: _____

VOLUNTARIO 1: _____

VOLUNTARIO 2: _____

3. Uses of *por* and *para*

11-6 Testimonios. You work for a natural medicine company, Hierbas de Vida. Your bo
asks you to create an advertisement in which you present your clients' testimonials in ord
to reach out to other potential clients.

Paso 1. With a classmate, create a script in which three people present three different
testimonials about what herbal remedies did for them and what it meant to them. Use **por**
para as much as possible.

MODELO: *Testimonio:* Para la familia Rodríguez, los productos de Hierbas de Vida
                        realmente cambiaron su vida. El Sr. Rodríguez, que sufría dolores
                        cabeza terribles, por el precio de 5.00 pesos, compró un día unas
                        gotas para la migraña.

                        Sr. Rodríguez: Tomé el remedio dos veces por día y, por primera v
                        en una semana, pude levantarme temprano para ir al trabajo . . .

Testimonio 1:

_____

_____

_____

Testimonio 2:

_____

_____

_____

Testimonio 3:

_____

_____

_____

Paso 2. Now, with your classmate, act out one or two testimonials for the whole class.

4. Relative pronouns

11-7 En el centro médico. You are working at the university health center this semester as a medical student in practice. The chief nurse shows you around and explains who's who at the center, what the procedures are, and identifies objects. With a classmate, create a dialog in which the student points out objects and people, asking questions about them. The nurse will answer, giving plenty of specific details. Make sure you review the section on relative pronouns on page 384 of your textbook.

MODELO: ESTUDIANTE: ¿Para qué sirve este papel?
            ENFERMERO/A: Éste es el papel que deben rellenar los enfermos que llegan a
                    urgencias.
            ESTUDIANTE: Y ¿quiénes son las dos personas que están en la recepción?
            ENFERMERO/A: La mujer que lleva una bata azul es Raquel, la enfermera de
                    noche, quien es también mi compañera de cuarto; la mujer con
                    quien habla Raquel es Pilar, que es pediatra.

Diálogo

ESTUDIANTE: _____

ENFERMERO/A: _____

ESTUDIANTE: _____

ENFERMERO/A: _____

ESTUDIANTE: _____

ENFERMERO/A: _____

ESTUDIANTE: _____

ENFERMERO/A: _____

ESTUDIANTE: _____

ENFERMERO/A: _____

ESTUDIANTE: _____

ENFERMERO/A: _____

ESTUDIANTE: _____

MOSAICOS

11-8 Crucigrama. The following crossword puzzle contains eight words related to health and sickness. Fill in the spaces with the help of the statements below. Review the vocabul. list on page 395 of your textbook to complete this exercise.

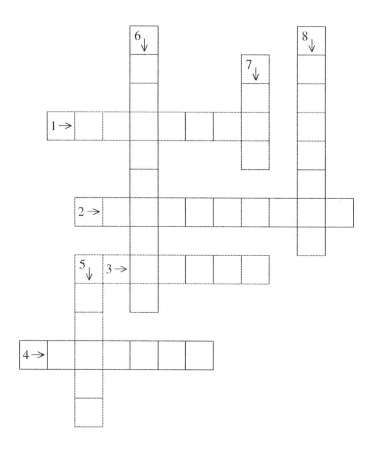

1. Los síntomas son: tos, nariz tapada y congestión.

2. Muchos niños la tienen de oídos y de garganta. Se trata con antibióticos.

3. ¡El de cabeza y el de muelas es terrible!

4. Es la temperatura demasiado alta del cuerpo humano, por un problema de salud.

5. Hay vacunas para prevenirla en el invierno.

6. Es la reacción al picor de nariz.

7. Es la reacción al picor o al dolor de garganta.

8. Si la tienes muy alta, debes hacer dieta, ejercicio, dieta y visitar al cardiólogo.

11-9 Las dietas de moda. The class will be divided into two teams: those who are firm believers in a low-carb, high-protein diet and those who defend a low-fat, whole-grain diet. If you are not familiar with these different types of weight management diets, do some basic research on health web pages and weight-loss program pages such as http://www.weightwatchers.com (mainly for a low-fat, low-protein diet) and http://www.atkins.com (for a low-carb, high-protein diet).

Paso 1. Each team will brainstorm to come up with recommended/forbidden foods and eating habits for the diet they are defending as the most successful way to lose weight.

COMIDAS RECOMENDADAS	COMIDAS PROHIBIDAS	HÁBITOS ALIMENTICIOS

Paso 2. The two teams will present:

1. Reasons to lose weight: Describe symptoms that may suggest a weight problem.

2. Recommendations/prohibitions for following the diet: Include what (not) to eat and when.

3. The types of people with health issues and lifestyles for whom this diet is (not) recommended: Make sure you incorporate all the grammar points studied in the chapter.

Paso 3. After the presentation, each team will question two aspects of the other team's diet; each team will then present their arguments for their position.

ENFOQUE CULTURAL

11-10 Una experiencia terrible.

Estudiante A: You are spending a semester abroad in the Dominican Republic. Two days ago at the beach, you were stung by a rare fish and developed a terrible allergic reaction. Your family took you to a hospital, and then to a natural healer. At the moment, you are recovering at home and decide to write an e-mail to your best friend in the States relating your experience with modern as well as traditional medicine in this Caribbean country.

Estudiante B: You receive an e-mail from your best friend, who is spending a semester abroad in the Dominican Republic. Your friend suffered a terrible reaction to a sting and needed medical attention. Write back expressing sympathy and opinions about his or her experience with traditional and modern medicine.

Nota: This activity can be done as an on-line chat activity in a language lab.

11-11 Medicina natural vs. medicina moderna. Cuba has an impressive medical system based on western medical and technological advances. However, traditional, natural, and alternative medical approaches are becoming popular again among Cubans. With a group of students, do some basic research on the Cuban medical system and on traditional and alternative medicine; you should describe and compare the two approaches to healing. Present your results to the class. You can access the following website: http://www.sld.cu/sitios/mednat/ or http://salud.cibercuba.com

You can do a search on the following topics:

medicina tradicional cubana

medicina alternativa cubana

sistema médico cubano

ministerio de sanidad cubano

11-12 Nuevo cine cubano. In the past fifteen years, Cuban films have become popular in Spanish-speaking countries as well as in the United States. Some of these movies are *Fresa y Chocolate* and *Guantanamera.* Other famous movies 'such as *Buena Vista Social Club*' portray Cuban life and culture, and the Spanish movie *Cosas que dejé en la Habana* is about Cuban exiles in Spain.

Paso 1. Do some basic research on these movies and their directors, as well as on the Cuban film industry. Create a short presentation on one film director, a period of Cuban film history, or two recent Cuban movies. Present the information you found to the class. Useful websites: http://www.cubacine.cu or http://www.cubaculture.com.

Paso 2. If you have an opportunity, view a Cuban movie or a segment of it, and talk in class about the plot, the characters, and the life this movie portrays. How are the themes/characters/plots different from or similar to those of American movies you have seen?

...●●●●●●●...

CAPÍTULO

12

¡Buen viaje!

A PRIMERA VISTA

12-1 Formas de viajar. Paso 1. With a classmate, decide on the reasons to choose one type of transportation over another and why.

TRANSPORTE	VENTAJAS	DESVENTAJAS	CIRCUNSTANCIAS
coche			
moto			
tren			
avión			
autobús			
autocar (autobús de largo recorrido)			
metro			
barco			

Now, discuss the types of travel accommodation you prefer, under what circumstances, a
the advantages and disadvantages of each.

ALOJAMIENTO	VENTAJAS	DESVENTAJAS	CIRCUNSTANC
hotel de lujo			
hostal o pensión			
albergue juvenil			
camping			
apartamento			

Paso 2. Get together with another pair and discuss your answers. Do you have differing
opinions? Write a short paragraph in which you give your opinion on the best way to trave

12-2 Itinerarios creativos. Create three itineraries to a Spanish-speaking country based on these three categories: **viaje de lujo**, **viaje de aventura**, and **viaje cultural**.

Paso 1. With a classmate, decide how you would travel to the region, how you would travel within the region, and what types of accommodation you would arrange.

Viaje de Lujo

LUGAR	TRANSPORTE	ALOJAMIENTO	TRANSPORTE INTERNO	ACTIVIDADES

Viaje de Aventura

LUGAR	TRANSPORTE	ALOJAMIENTO	TRANSPORTE INTERNO	ACTIVIDADES

Viaje Cultural

LUGAR	TRANSPORTE	ALOJAMIENTO	TRANSPORTE INTERNO	ACTIVIDAI

Paso 2. Create a brochure in which you present the three alternatives to a potential traveler Make sure you give information about activities and places to go to within the region.

_____

_____

_____

_____

_____

_____

_____

_____

_____

_____

_____

_____

_____

_____

_____

_____

_____

_____

_____

_____

_____

_____

Nombre: _____   **Fecha:** _____

12-3 Yo me bajo en la próxima . . . With a classmate, find a map of a Spanish-speaking city's transportation system (metro in Madrid: http://www.metromadrid.es; metro in Mexi City: http://www.metro.df.gob.mx/; metro in Caracas: http://www.metrodecaracas.com.ve Print out a map and ask your classmate questions about how to get from one subway statio to another. Your classmate should respond with commands and recommendations. Exchar roles.

FUNCIONES Y FORMAS

1. Subjunctive in adjective clauses

12-4 Encuesta. Is there anybody who does things this way? You will ask a group of five students if anybody does the following and report on their responses. Follow the model.

viajar a europa en barco	montar en globo
venir a la clase en motocicleta	no llevar reservaciones de hotel cuando viaja
montar en bicicleta por la playa	alojarse en albergues juveniles
viajar en una limusina	dormir en la playa
salir por la noche con chófer	llevar sólo una bolsa de mano de equipaje

MODELO: Viajar a Latinoamérica todos los veranos

E1: *¿Hay alguien que viaje a Latinoamérica todos los veranos?*
E2: *No, no viajamos a Latinoamérica todos los veranos.*

o:
E2: *Sí, yo viajo a México en junio para visitar a mi hermano, que vive en Monterrey.*

Informe:
E1: *En nuestro grupo no hay nadie que viaje a Latinoamérica todos los veranos. /En nuestro grupo hay una persona que viaja a México todos los veranos.*

12-5 Aquí no hay quien viva. You live in a very busy part of town with a lot of people, traffic, and noise. Your neighbors are terribly rowdy, the building management is bad, and you keep complaining. You decide to ask your landlord about this situation, and he will answer your complaints.

Your complaints:

¡Aquí no hay quien duerma por las noches!

¡Aquí no hay quien aparque el coche por las tardes!

¡Aquí no hay quien se pueda duchar con agua caliente por las mañanas!

¡Aquí no hay quien arregle el ascensor del edificio!

¡Aquí no hay quien camine sin miedo por la noche a su casa!

¡Aquí no hay quien recoja las basuras del edificio todos los días!

Now, ask your landlord (*casero*) your questions.

MODELO: ¡Aquí no hay quien apague la televisión antes de la 1:00 de la madrugada!
        TÚ: *¿Hay alguien en el edificio que se acueste antes de la medianoche?*
   CASERO: *No, no hay nadie que se acueste antes de la 1:00 de madrugada, porque todos los vecinos son estudiantes.*

2. Possessive pronouns

3. Stressed possessive adjectives

12-6 Mío, tuyo o suyo. You are sorting things out in your basement. You and your roommate are trying to figure out what belongs to you, to you and your roommate, and to your neighbors. Create a dialog in which you decide on the following items:

una mochila roja y una mochila gris	cuatro sillas y una mesa
una aspiradora amarilla y una negra	tres llantas de coche
dos cascos de montar en bicicleta	tres bicicletas de carreras
una máquina de cortar la hierba	un par de botas de esquiar del número 47
tres cajas de libros	tres pares de esquís
un sofá-cama	¿. . .? (add other items)

MODELO: E1: *Oye, estas dos mochilas son nuestras, ¿verdad?*
        E2: *Sí, la roja es la mochila mía y la gris es la tuya.*
        E1: *Y la bicicleta tuya es la de carreras blanca y negra, ¿verdad?*
        E2: *No, ésa es de los vecinos, y ese casco rojo es suyo también. La bicicleta mía es la roja.*

E1: _____

E2: _____

E1: _____

E2: _____

E1: _____

E2: _____

E1: _____

E2: _____

E1: _____

E2: _____

E1: _____

E2: _____

4. Review of the preterit and imperfect

12-7 El transporte en los tiempos de antes. How did people travel in the past? What methods did they use to get from one place to another, near or far? How long did it take to arrive at destinations? With a classmate or a group of students, discuss how your parents, your grandparents and your great-grandparents traveled when they were young.

Paso 1. Make a list of different modes of transportation, the places people went, and how long it took them to get there.

TRANSPORTE	DESTINOS	TIEMPO DE VIAJE

Paso 2. Write a brief narrative in which you tell about a trip that someone in your family took in the past. Use preterit and imperfect. Make sure to compare this trip—the mode of travel, the time it took, etc.—with how you might make the same trip today.

Un viaje del pasado

_____

_____

_____

_____

_____

_____

_____

_____

_____

_____

_____

MOSAICOS

12-8 SOPA DE LETRAS. Find eight words related to airports in the following word puzzle. Then complete the sentences with the appropriate words. Review the vocabulary list on page 429 of your textbook to complete this exercise.

J	K	L	Y	T	R	C	R	I	G	P	T
E	A	H	M	N	K	E	B	F	H	P	U
Z	D	Q	W	B	D	Q	S	S	R	R	R
V	U	E	L	O	V	U	T	P	U	P	I
X	A	B	X	A	V	I	W	O	E	D	S
T	N	A	V	C	P	P	Y	L	P	R	T
T	A	R	J	E	T	A	Q	E	K	R	A
N	Q	J	T	P	G	J	R	T	Y	H	K
I	D	F	J	S	D	E	S	T	I	N	O
P	A	S	A	P	O	R	T	E	D	B	Q
Z	H	G	Y	W	U	Y	T	G	M	W	K

1. Se necesita una _____ de embarque para subir al avión.

2. Hay un control de _____ en todos los aeropuertos internacionales.

3. El avión con _____ a Bogotá salió desde Houston.

4. Mi _____ es el Iberia 506, de Miami a Valencia.

5. La sala de _____ en el aeropuerto de Caracas estaba llena de gente.

6. La aerolínea perdió mi _____.

7. En la _____ los oficiales registran las maletas.

8. Yo viajo siempre en clase _____ porque es más económica.

12-9 Taller creativo. Romances del metro. In pairs or groups of three, create a poem (e a haiku) or a short story based on a brief romantic encounter on a subway. What kinds of platonic encounters may occur? Do you believe in serendipity?

Situaciones posibles:

• Dos personas que se ven todos los días en el metro pero nunca se hablan . . .

• Dos personas que se tropiezan (*bump into each other*) al entrar y al salir del vagón . . .

• Dos personas que se re-encuentran después de mucho tiempo sin verse . . .

Brainstorm two more situations:

• _____ . . .

• _____ . . .

Your poem or story must be written in the past; use the preterit and imperfect.

_____

_____

_____

_____

_____

_____

_____

_____

_____

_____

_____

_____

_____

_____

ENFOQUE CULTURAL

12-10 El ecoturismo en Costa Rica. Paso 1. Do some basic research on ecotourism in Costa Rica. You may use the following websites listed below, or do your own Internet search. Make a list of three activities you would like to do in Costa Rica and include their locations, costs and other pertinent details.

http://www.travelexcellence.com/ecotourism2.htm ;
http://www.ahorre.com/ecotourism/Costa_Rica_Travel.htm

ACTIVIDAD	LUGAR	COSTO	DETALLES
_____	_____	_____	_____
_____	_____	_____	_____
_____	_____	_____	_____

Paso 2. Now get together with a classmate to compare the information you found. Are you interested in any of the same activities? Which ones? Choose one that you are both interested in and imagine that you went to Costa Rica and participated in this activity. Write a brief paragraph in which you tell about what you did, what it was like, where in Costa Rica it was etc. Use the preterit and the imperfect. Present your paragraph to the class and enhance it with some photos of ecotourism in Costa Rica.

Nuestra experiencia con el ecoturismo en Costa Rica

_____

_____

_____

_____

_____

_____

_____

_____

_____

_____

_____

_____

_____

_____

Nombre: _____   Fecha: _____

12-11 Navegando por el Canal de Panamá. Paso 1. Do some basic research on the Canal de Panamá: its geographical location, its extension, rivers that flow into it, points of interest, and the names of its main locks (**esclusas**) and reservoirs (**embalses**). Also, examine the way in which its engineering system allows ships to sail through it. List the information you find.

ubicación: _____

extensión: _____

ríos y mares: _____

puntos de interés: _____

esclusas y embalses: _____

funcionamiento: _____

Paso 2. With a classmate, recreate a possible trip from the Pacific Ocean (give the name of the port of departure) to the Caribbean Sea (give the name of the port of exit). Be specific about the places you will pass, how the ship will sail from one point to the next, etc. You will find information on the Canal at http://www.pancanal.com Add a map for your trip itinerary.

Un viaje por el Canal

MAPA

CAPÍTULO

13

Las artes y las letras

A PRIMERA VISTA

13-1 Artistas famosos. Paso 1. Find more information about the following famous people. Give their country of origin, their profession, and their artistic achievements. Some of these people have their own webpage. Make sure you look at them.

	PAÍS	PROFESIÓN	LOGROS ARTÍSTICOS
Alejandro Amenábar			
Sara Baras			
Gael García Bernal			
Laura Restrepo			
Carlos Nuñez			
Daniel Barenboim			
Alfonso Cuarón			

Paso 2. Choose the two artists from the list that interest you most and write a brief biogra[phy] of each. Then, with a classmate, share the information you have found and tell him/her wh[at] you would ask these artists if you could interview them. Use the conditional.

ARTISTAS

_____   _____

_____   _____

_____   _____

_____   _____

_____   _____

_____   _____

_____   _____

_____   _____

_____   _____

_____   _____

_____   _____

_____   _____

_____   _____

13-2 Un gaitero internacional. Carlos Nuñez is a famous musician from Galicia, Spain. G[o] to his website (http://www.carlos-nunez.com) and under "music," view his 10-minute vide[o] clip entitled *EPK Mayo Longo.* If this video clip is not available, you can view *Cómo se grabó mayo longo,* a short video about how he recorded this song, at http://www.youtube.com/watch?v=AYWvCE3ktyY.

Paso 1. Listen to Carlos Nuñez's music and his interview, and look at his webpage.

1. Describe al artista. Escribe seis adjetivos que describen su apariencia física y su
    personalidad.

    _____

    _____

    _____

2. ¿Cómo describirías el estilo musical del artista? Según el artista, ¿cómo ha cambiado su
    estilo musical y sus grabaciones en los últimos años? ¿Cómo han sido sus conciertos?
    Puedes encontrar esta información en las entrevistas (*video clips*) y en otras secciones de
    la página web.

    _____

    _____

    _____

3. ¿Dónde ha tocado Carlos Nuñez? ¿Con qué otros músicos famosos ha tocado el artista?

    _____

    _____

    _____

4. ¿Sabes cuál será su calendario de conciertos para los próximos meses?

    _____

    _____

    _____

    Compare the information you obtained with that of other students and of the whole class.

Nombre: _____   Fecha: _____

Paso 2. Now, with a classmate, you will think of another artist or famous person from Spa
or Latin America. Find a personal webpage, and present information to the class on this
celebrity following the format of the questions in Paso 1.

Personaje: _____

1. _____

_____

_____

2. _____

_____

_____

3. _____

_____

_____

4. _____

_____

_____

13-3 ¡Feliz cumpleaños! In 1605, the famous novel *Don Quijote de la Mancha* was first published, and its 400th anniversary has been widely celebrated in the Spanish-speaking world.

Paso 1. Find basic information about the plot of the novel. Who are the main characters and what is the plot? Also, present some basic information on Miguel de Cervantes, the author of *Don Quijote de la Mancha.*

Trama (*plot*):

_____

_____

_____

_____

Personajes principales:

_____

_____

_____

_____

Autor:

_____

_____

_____

_____

Paso 2. Investigate further by reading more about the plot, or by reading a short passage f
the novel. Summarize one of the adventures in which Don Quijote and Sancho Panza becc
involved: What happened, who were the characters involved, and how did the adventure e
You can find information in many of the books at your local or college library. Much
information is also available on the Internet.

Resumen de una escena o aventura de Don Quijote y Sancho Panza:

_____

_____

_____

_____

Paso 3. Create a short dialog using your own words between Don Quijote and the characte
of the scene or story you just related above. Recreate the main encounter and give voice to
the characters!

Diálogo entre Don Quijote y _____

_____

_____

_____

_____

_____

_____

_____

FUNCIONES Y FORMAS

1. Affirmative and negative expressions

13-4 Eventos culturales. You arrive in a Spanish-speaking city and go to the tourist information office to get some basic information about cultural events. You are interested in going to the theater, seeing a movie, and listening to music during your stay.

Paso 1. With a classmate, create a dialogue in which . . .

1. you ask the tourist information person about cultural events that will be taking place during your stay;

2. the tourist information employee answers negatively to most of your inquiries.

TURISTA: _____

EMPLEADO/A: _____

TURISTA: _____

EMPLEADO/A: _____

TURISTA: _____

EMPLEADO/A: _____

TURISTA: _____

EMPLEADO/A: _____

TURISTA: _____

EMPLEADO/A: _____

TURISTA: _____

Nombre: _____   Fecha: _____

Paso 2. After your day in this city, you engage in conversation that evening with another tourist at a café. Respond to the following statements given by your new friend, using **también** and **tampoco**, and explaining in detail what you did.

1. Pasé todo el día participando en diferentes eventos culturales por la ciudad. ¿Y tú?

   _____

2. Pude ver el museo de arte contemporáneo. ¿Y tú?

   _____

3. El único modo de transporte que encontré fue un taxi. ¿Y tú?

   _____

4. Fui al Palacio de los Reyes porque hoy es el único día que está abierto. ¿Y tú?

   _____

5. Entré en muchas tiendas y gasté dinero en comprar ropa. ¿Y tú?

   _____

6. Monté en las barcas del lago del parque para pasar el tiempo. ¿Y tú?

   _____

7. Fui a una presentación de baile flamenco. ¿Y tú?

   _____

2. Subjunctive with expressions of doubt

13-5 El sábado por la noche. Your friend/spouse/fiancé(e) is very picky when it comes to entertainment. Every time you make a suggestion about what to do on Saturday night —see a play, go to a concert, a new restaurant, etc. —he/she questions whether or not it will be interesting or boring, too expensive, etc. Using expressions of doubt, create a dialogue in which you present your best ideas on what to do and where to go, and the other person expresses doubts about them.

TÚ: _____

ÉL/ELLA: _____

TÚ: _____

ÉL/ELLA: _____

TÚ: _____

ÉL/ELLA: _____

TÚ: _____

ÉL/ELLA: _____

TÚ: _____

ÉL/ELLA: _____

13-6 "Mala espina." Your friend has invited you and your family to a dinner theater where you previously had a bad experience because the food was bad and the play was not very interesting. You have your doubts about the quality of the food, the service, and the entertainment. Your friend will present statements and reasons for his or her choice. You will respond with doubts and disbelief about these statements.

MODELO: E1: *El chef es nuevo y es francés.*
          E2: *Dudo que este chef sea mejor que el anterior, y no creo que los chefs franceses cocinen mejor que los chefs paraguayos.*
          E1: *El drama es un misterio y es muy interesante.*
          E2: *No creo que el drama pueda ser más interesante que el último que vi.*

3. The conditional

13-7 Fantasías. Imagine that you are in the following places located in different Spanish speaking cities. Do some research either in the *Enfoque cultural* of previous chapters in yo textbook or on the Internet. List at least three activities you would do.

¿Qué harías en los siguientes lugares?

1. las cataratas del Salto del Ángel, en Venezuela, con tu familia de vacaciones

_____

_____

_____

2. el barrio de San Telmo, en Buenos Aires, con amigos, por la noche

_____

_____

_____

3. el Mercado de El Rastro en Madrid, en tu tiempo libre durante tu semestre en España

_____

_____

_____

4. el Museo del Oro, en Bogotá, en un viaje de investigación

_____

_____

_____

5.   el parque natural El Yunque en Puerto Rico, en un trabajo de verano temporal

_____

_____

_____

6.   la casa-museo de Frida Kahlo (*Casa Azul*), en México, D.F., para una clase de pintura

_____

_____

_____

13-8 ¡Megafantasía! Choosing one of the situations listed above, create a **megafantasía** with your classmates. In groups of six students, develop a hypothetical story based on one of these situations, taking turns in writing one thing each of you would do.

Procedimiento: Student 1 will write one hypothetical action; student 2 will read student 1's sentence or paragraph and write a continuation of it, with another hypothetical action; the story will continue until student 6 writes the ending. The group will read it together, exchange it with those of other groups, or read it aloud to the class. Have fun!

4. Reciprocal verbs and pronouns

13-9 Sentimientos recíprocos. The class will be divided into pairs.

Student A: You are having a difficult experience in a relationship with another person or with a group of people. You write a letter to a famous newspaper columnist to expose the problematic relationship(s) and to seek advice.

Student B: You are an advice columnist of a local newspaper. Readers write to you about difficult situations or personal problems. You answer with direct advice on how to better the situation. Respond to student A's letter, commanding the person to take certain actions with the people involved.

Nombre: _____   **Fecha:** _____

Estimado/a _____ :

_____
_____
_____
_____
_____
_____
_____
_____
_____
_____
_____
_____

                                         _____

Estimado/a _____ :

_____
_____
_____
_____
_____
_____
_____
_____
_____
_____
_____
_____

                                         _____

MOSAICOS

13-10 Parejas famosas. There are many famous couples in the Spanish-speaking world. Their celebrity may be seen in a historical, artistic, or popular cultural perspective, and their relationships may be of camaraderie, political ties, love, or friendship. Some examples include the following:

- Federico García Lorca —Salvador Dalí

- Hernán Cortés —Doña Mariana, "La Malinche"

- Isabel la Católica —Fernando el Católico

- Frida Kahlo —Diego Rivera

- Fidel Castro —Ernesto "Che" Guevara

- Can you think of another one?

Do some research on each person in the relationship, if possible. Find out why they are famous in the first place. Then, find out what type of relationship they had (friendship, marriage, political ties) and write a report in which you present the information you researched.

13-11 Una sevillana. A popular **sevillana** song (a type of flamenco song) speculates abou
world without money. The following verses are an adaptation of this popular song.

Dinero, dinero, dinero . . .

¡Qué bonito sería el mundo

Si no existiera el dinero!

Si no existiera el dinero

No habría tanta falsedad (*falseness*),

Todos seríamos más buenos.

¿Crees que es verdad? ¿Cómo sería el mundo sin dinero?

Continue this song, writing another set of lines. Make the lines rhyme. You can start with t
last line above.

Todos seríamos más buenos . . .

_____

_____

_____

_____,

Pero yo si que te digo:

¡Qué bonito sería el mundo

si no existiera el dinero!

13-12 Ensalada de palabras. The following word puzzle contains the most famous literary beginning ever written in Spanish literature. It has been started for you. Can you find it? Who wrote it?

G	K	E	N	O	Q	J	U	N	L	V	G	L	U	G	A	R	P	O	T	X	R
D	E	K	J	G	L	A	B	V	X	U	M	A	N	C	H	A	I	F	Y	Z	E
D	E	H	Y	Z	X	C	U	Y	O	L	G	W	R	N	O	M	B	R	E	P	W
L	N	O	I	Y	Q	U	I	E	R	O	H	L	A	C	O	R	D	A	R	M	E

Frase: *En un lugar . . .* _____

_____

Obra: _____

Autor: _____

ENFOQUE CULTURAL

13-13 Premios Príncipe de Asturias. Every year, the Spanish foundation Fundación Príncipe de Asturias presents its awards to honor scientific and humanistic endeavors. Wit group of students, visit the website http://www.fpa.es, the official webpage of the Fundaci Príncipe de Asturias.

Paso 1. Go to *Premiados*, and find out about the different prize categories presented every year, and who/what has obtained recognition during the past few years.

Premios Príncipe de Asturias		
CATEGORÍAS	**AÑOS**	**GALARDONADOS**

Paso 2. Choose one person, and one institution or cultural icon, and write a report stating th reasons for this recognition.

Premio _____ *Gardonado/a* _____ *Año* _____

_____

_____

_____

_____

_____

13-14 Diarios de motocicleta en Bolivia. View the movie *Diarios de motocicleta* about Che Guevara and the experience he had with a friend traveling through South America that informed him politically. Pay close attention to the scenes in which he visits Bolivia. Write a paragraph describing these scenes, including where he went, why, with whom, and what he saw and thought. How did Che Guevara's experience in Bolivia contribute to his political ideals and beliefs?

CAPÍTULO

14

Los cambios sociales

A PRIMERA VISTA

14-1 La población de los países hispanos. Access the website http://www.guiadelmundo.com, and choose four countries not shown in the statistical presentation in *Cambios en la sociedad* on page 467, for example, Paraguay, Peru, Costa Rica, Honduras.

Paso 1. Select the category **Población** on the website. Provide the basic information about the country's population that the chart below calls for. Present this information to a group of students.

paises →			
población			
crecimiento			
divisiones étnicas			
porcentajes hombres/mujeres			
esperanza de vida			
alfabetismo			

Paso 2. With a group of students, choose two countries from the ones you presented. Compare the data and write a brief report in which you present the descriptive information about them.

_____

_____   _____
_____   _____
_____   _____
_____   _____
_____   _____
_____   _____
_____   _____
_____   _____
_____   _____
_____   _____

14-2 Mapa lingüístico del español. Spanish-speaking populations are growing rapidly in the United States. For this activity, you will access the website http://www.mla.org, the official site for the Modern Language Association.

Paso 1.

- Click on the MLA Language Map link.

- Select Spanish as the language to research.

- Select an area of the country you want to find more information about (your hometown, your university town, the county, etc.). You can select by state, county, or zip code. Find out how many people speak Spanish in your area. Research several towns and major cities of a region. Present the numbers in terms of total population, Spanish-speaking population, and other languages spoken in that area.

AREA	NO. DE HABITANTES	NO. DE HISPANOHABLANTES	NO. DE HABLANTES DE OTRA LENGUA

Paso 2. After sharing your data with two or three classmates, write a short report in which you present the results to the class.

_____

_____

_____

_____

_____

_____

_____

_____

_____

_____

_____

14-3 Las mujeres de tu casa. Do you know the history of your family's female relatives? Talk to different women in your family and find out more about your female ancestors and your living female relatives. You may find out, for instance, that your grandmother was the first woman in your family to hold a job, or that a female relative was involved in politics!

Paso 1. Use the information you obtained to present a female genealogy to a group of students.

Points of interest:

- ethnic background

- education level

- professional development

- political, social, religious activity

- other relevant topics

Paso 2. Write a letter to a family member in which you present the female side of your family. Use it as a special occasion letter, for instance, as a birthday gift to a sibling, parent, or some other relative!

Querido/a _____ :

_____

_____

_____

_____

_____

_____

_____

_____

_____

_____

_____

Un saludo de

_____

FUNCIONES Y FORMAS

1. Adverbial conjunctions that require the subjunctive

14-4 Violencia doméstica. Domestic violence is a current problem in modern society. Spanish-speaking newspapers report cases of domestic violence generally against women. Look for Spanish-speaking newspapers that talk about this problem or related cases of mistreatment of 'or violence against' women.

Paso 1. Complete the following activities.

1. Escribe un resumen de la noticia:

_____

_____

_____

2. ¿Cuál es el problema que se presenta en la noticia? ¿Es éste un problema común en los Estados Unidos? ¿Por qué crees que sí o no? ¿Crees que afecta a ciertos grupos sociales comunidades más que a otros?

_____

_____

_____

Comparte tus opiniones con otros estudiantes en la clase.

Paso 2. With a classmate, give an oral presentation of the problems modern society deals with regarding discrimination and violence against women.

First, present the problem. If it is specific to a region or a social group, make sure you speci this point.

Second, give concrete solutions and prepare a plan derived from the news you found, presenting what needs to be done for society to solve this problem.

Make sure you use the structures studied in section 1 of *Funciones y formas* on pages 474–475 of your textbook.

2. Adverbial conjunctions that take the subjunctive or the indicative

14-5 Los hispanos y la sociedad estadounidense. Find information in several Spanish-speaking newspapers regarding relevant issues that affect Hispanics as a community in the United States. An example of an electronic Hispanic news source is http://www.laraza.com, but many cities and regions have their own local Hispanic magazines or newspapers.

Paso 1. With a classmate, list five issues that impact the lives of Hispanics in the United States. These can be related to education, health, politics, economics, etc. Make a list using the headings in the chart below.

PROBLEMA Y LUGAR	CONDICIONES	SOLUCIONES

Paso 2. Present two issues to another pair. Follow these guidelines.

1. Present the situation, its past and its present. Give specific details as to how and when certain things occurred.

2. Describe what can happen (or not) in the future under certain conditions, or provided that certain conditions and solutions occur.

Make sure you review sections 1 and 2 of *Funciones y formas* on pages 474–478 of your textbook.

Paso 3. Write a short editorial for a local newspaper (your school newspaper, a regional cultural magazine) in which you present one of these issues and possible future solutions, conditions, or demands you consider important for the well-being of the community.

_____
_____
_____
_____
_____
_____
_____
_____
_____
_____
_____

14-6 La voz pública. Lately, a number of men and women of Hispanic origin have been appointed to important political or economic positions in the national administration and financial and local institutions: political aides, local politicians, social advocates, heads of corporations, etc. Do some research on Hispanic public figures in your community, region, state. In this activity, you will personify a real public figure (Hispanic if possible): a social advocate, a local politician, etc.

Present your agenda to a group of students. Name three issues that, according to you, need solutions or new approaches. Present your future actions, provided that certain conditions a in place.

Answer questions from your audience.

3. The past perfect

14-7 Mujeres increíbles. The following are brief biographies of four important female figures of Hispanic literature: Sor Juana Inés de la Cruz (México), Rosalía de Castro (Galicia, Spain), Gabriela Mistral (Chile), and Alfonsina Storni (Argentina).

Paso 1. Read the following biographies and write four things each of these women writers had already done by a certain age.

> Rosalía de Castro nació en Santiago de Compostela, España, en 1837 y murió en 1885. Escribió sus primeros versos a los 12 años. A los 17 años era conocida como una gran escritora entre sus amigos y sus conocidos. Rosalía se casó y tuvo el primer hijo un año después de su matrimonio. En total tuvo 6 hijos, pero todos murieron antes que ella. Rosalía de Castro murió de cáncer con 48 años. Aunque escribió en gallego, también lo hizo en castellano. En su poesía describe el sentimiento de la gente gallega. Se la considera la gran representante de las letras gallegas y de las mujeres escritoras de su tiempo.

> Gabriela Mistral nació en Chile. Su padre abandonó a la familia cuando Gabriela tenía 3 años. A los 15 años publicó sus primeras poesías en un periódico. En 1910 comenzó a trabajar como maestra, y recibió los primeros premios por su poesía. A partir de 1925, viajó a Europa donde fue Cónsul de su país en Nápoles y en Lisboa. Fue la primera escritora latinoamericana que recibió el Premio Nobel, en 1945. En 1954 viajó a Nueva York. Murió allí en 1957. En su poesía, los temas de la niñez, la maternidad y la mujer siempre están presentes.

> Sor Juana Inés de la Cruz nació en 1651 en San Miguel de Nepantla, en México. Cuando tenía 3 años ya sabía leer y escribir. Cuando era todavía una niña compuso sus primeros versos religiosos. Fue monja desde los 16 años, y en su corta vida fue amiga y confidente de importantes personajes de la cultura y la política de su tiempo. Sin embargo, la iglesia no veía bien su carrera literaria. El Obispo de Puebla insistió en que Sor Juana dejara de escribir. Entonces, en 1691, Sor Juana le obedeció y vendió los cuatro mil libros de su biblioteca, todos sus instrumentos científicos y musicales y dedicó el dinero a obras de caridad. Murió el 17 de abril de 1695, durante una epidemia de cólera en su convento. Su poesía es alegre y rica, y en ella se defiende la capacidad de pensamiento y análisis de las mujeres.

Alfonsina Storni nació en un cantón suizo el 22 de mayo de 1892, pero fue a vivir a Argentina cuando tenía 4 años, y vivió en varias ciudades de este país. En 1938, se suicidó la Playa de la Perla, ahogándose en el mar. En su poesía, siempre quiso afirmar el papel de mujer en la sociedad como un ser que piensa, que analiza, y no sólo desempeña los papele de esposa y madre. Publicó siete libros de poemas, y el último lo publicó en el año de su muerte.

1. _____

_____

_____

_____

2. _____

_____

_____

_____

3. _____

_____

_____

_____

4. _____

_____

_____

_____

Paso 2. From the above authors, choose one that especially interests you. Look for a poem by her, bring it to class, and read it aloud to your classmates.

1. ¿Cuáles son las palabras conocidas del poema? Subraya (*Underline*) todas las palabras familiares de este poema.

    _____

    _____

2. ¿Cuáles son las palabras más importantes del poema?

    _____

    _____

3. ¿Puedes especular cuál es el mensaje principal de este poema? ¿el tema?

    _____

    _____

4. ¿Tiene el poema una rima (*rhyme*) clara? ¿Es el tono del poema triste/alegre/divertido/ligero/oscuro?

    _____

    _____

5. Escribe tres adjetivos que pueden describir, en tu opinión, el "sentimiento" que produce este poema en tus compañeros y en ti.

    _____

    _____

Paso 3. Find out more about the author of your poem. Compile the information and tell your group biographical as well as literary information about the poet.

4. The infinitive as subject or object

14-8 Los retos sociales. The class will be divided into several groups of three to five students. Each group will debate about the following social issues that affect modern societies, both in Spanish-speaking countries and in the United States.

Paso 1. For each issue, decide what position you will take. Then, under **A favor** or **En contra**, write adjectives that describe your position: **intolerable**, **importante**, **deseable** . .

SITUACIÓN	A FAVOR	EN CONTRA
legalizar los matrimonios gay		
rebajar la edad en el consumo de alcohol		
legalizar la prostitución		
adoptar niños de otras razas		
utilizar símbolos y frases religiosos en actos públicos		
utilizar células-madre en la investigación científica		

Paso 2. Express your opinion in front of the group or the class, stating your arguments.

MODELO: *Al rebajar la edad del consumo de alcohol, más jóvenes tendrán acceso a bebid* *alcohólicas, y esto creará una situación incontrolable.*
O:
Rebajar la edad del consumo de alcohol es importante porque significa desmitificar (demystify) el tabú del alcohol entre los jóvenes.

MOSAICOS

14-9 Planes futuros.

Student A: You are spending time on a peace mission in a remote place thousands of miles away from your home, your friends, and most importantly, your fiancé(e). You write a long letter with all your plans for the time when you are back. You also have some fears that your fiancé(e) will have different plans for you two, or that feelings may have changed over time and distance. Write about all these plans for your return, and also express your reservations.

Student B: Your fiancé(e) is in the military on a peace mission and writes you a letter. He/she tells you of all the things you will do together once he or she is back home. Respond to him or her giving good wishes, and stating what is important to do to get back to your normal lives. Make sure you review grammar sections 1 and 2 of *Funciones y formas* on pages 474–478 of your textbook.

Queridísimo/a _____ :

_____

_____

_____

_____

_____

_____

_____

_____

_____

_____

_____

_____

_____

_____

_____

_____

_____

14-10 El voto hispano. You work for the local government as a translator and interpreter
Hispanics in your community. It is election time, and you are invited to a Spanish-speakin
television show to encourage Hispanics to vote and to explain the voting system to the
public.

Paso 1. With a classmate, list all the actions that you consider important when voting.

Consideraciones al votar:

_____

_____

_____

_____

_____

_____

_____

_____

_____

Paso 2. Now, create a script in which you present the information above, making sure you
give clear directions about what practices are allowed or forbidden, what is important, wha
is necessary, etc. Also, encourage certain groups to vote, such as women, youth, the elderly
presenting compelling reasons for their action. If relevant, give information on what
happened in past election years regarding the Hispanic vote compared to this election year.
(For instance: **En 1994 se habían registrado sólo 400 hispanos en el censo, pero este año
se han registrado casi 2.000.**)

Act out your script with a classmate for the class or a group of students. You and your
partner will play the parts of the invited guest and the television show host.

ENFOQUE CULTURAL

14-11 Los sistemas políticos. Do some basic research on the political history of Chile and the current political situation in this country. Give a brief description of both of these including types of government, political leaders, military situations, etc. Present your research to the class.

CHILE AHORA: **CHILE ANTES:**

_____   _____

_____   _____

_____   _____

_____   _____

_____   _____

_____   _____

_____   _____

_____   _____

_____   _____

_____   _____

_____   _____

_____   _____

_____   _____

_____   _____

_____   _____

_____   _____

_____   _____

14-12 Otros sistemas políticos. Choose two Spanish-speaking countries with different political systems or political situations, and different political histories over the past 100 years. With a group of students, research the countries' current political situation, and give a brief description of their political system and their current political leaders. Then, present a short political history of the countries, comparing their development over the past century, and one or two current national issues that are having an impact in these countries' societies.

País: _____   *País:* _____

_____   _____

_____   _____

_____   _____

_____   _____

_____   _____

_____   _____

_____   _____

_____   _____

_____   _____

_____   _____

_____   _____

_____   _____

_____   _____

_____   _____

_____   _____

_____   _____

_____   _____

_____   _____

15

Hacia el futuro

Nombre: _____

Fecha: _____

A PRIMERA VISTA

15-1 Un mundo en peligro. With a classmate, look up information on endangered animal species in Spanish-speaking countries. Some of these species are the following.

- el oso pirenaico (España)

- el mono Cebus (Venezuela)

- el lince ibérico (España)

- el quetzal (Costa Rica)

- el jaguar (Costa Rica)

Paso 1. With a classmate, make a list of five other endangered species in other Latin American countries. Give as much detail as possible for the ones above and the ones you find, such as the number of animals left, their natural habitat (**montaña**, **selva**, **ríos**, **mar**), and the reason for their endangered situation.

ANIMAL	NÚMERO	HÁBITAT	PROBLEMA

Paso 2. Write a report in which you present solutions to the problem. What can we do to preserve the species?

INFORME
_____

15-2 Una reserva natural. There are vast natural reserves and protected spaces in Latin America. Find out more about the following natural areas (for more information, go to http://www.ecoturismolatino.com and http://www.guiadelmundo.com).

- Parque Internacional de la Amistad (Costa Rica/Panamá)

- Reserva de la Biosfera Delta del Paraná (Argentina)

- Parque Natural de Amacayacu (Colombia)

- Machu Picchu (Perú)

- Reserva Natural de Miraflor (Nicaragua)

Paso 1. Make a list of the main attractions of each place—their flora, fauna, natural resources, and other important information.

ÁREA	INFORMACIÓN DE INTERÉS
_____	_____
	_____
	_____
	_____
	_____
	_____
	_____
	_____
	_____
	_____
	_____
_____	_____
	_____
	_____
	_____
	_____
	_____
	_____

Nombre: _____   **Fecha:** _____

_____

_____

Nombre: _____   **Fecha:** _____

_____   _____

_____

_____

_____

_____

_____

_____

_____

_____

_____

_____   _____

_____

_____

_____

_____

_____

_____

_____

_____

_____

Paso 2. Choose one of the parks above and design an information page for an adventure travel agency. Give basic information, as well as advice on how to travel responsibly and ecologically.

_____
_____
_____
_____
_____
_____
_____
_____
_____
_____
_____
_____
_____
_____
_____
_____
_____
_____
_____
_____

15-3 Planificación urbana. Imagine that you are hired to design a prototype city for the twenty-first century, in a vast, untouched expanse of land. Everything will be new, so you can create a truly innovative and technologically advanced place. Make a list of basic public services, transportation systems, energy sources, dwellings, and components that a small city may need.

Nombre: _____   Fecha: _____

Paso 1. Make a list of services and components, plus their innovations.

SERVICIO	INNOVACIÓN

Paso 2. Present your design to a group of students orally. The most ecologically and technologically advanced and livable city will be chosen.

FUNCIONES Y FORMAS

1. The imperfect subjunctive

2. *If*-clauses

15-4 Recordando. Read again the short story by Borges, "El etnógrafo," on page 457 (*Capítulo 13*) of your textbook.

Paso 1. Narrate the story again in the past, stating who said what and asked to do what to whom, using verbs of influence, hope, wish, opinion, and impersonal phrases.

┌───┐

"El etnógrafo"—Un recuento

_____
_____
_____
_____
_____
_____
_____
_____
_____
_____
_____
_____
_____
_____
_____
_____
_____
_____
_____
_____

└───┘

Paso 2. With a classmate, brainstorm a sequel for the story. Speculate on the following questions:

- What did Murdock do after he left the professor's office?

- Did he ever go back to the tribe he studied?

- Did he ever obtain an academic job?

- Did he ever reveal "the secret" to anyone?

Write a story sequel in which you speculate how Murdock's life would continue after his experience, provided that certain conditions occurred.

El etnógrafo después del etnógrafo . . .

Si _____

_____

_____

_____

_____

_____

_____

_____

_____

_____

_____

15-5 Opiniones diferentes. Think of three or four important issues that impact the environment in your town or region, or, alternatively, think of current public debates related to technology or scientific research.

Paso 1. With a classmate you will decide on a current situation and how it can be resolved in the future (the solutions that need to be implemented to make the situation better).

MODELO: *El reciclaje de pilas* (batteries) *y el uso de pilas recargables*
Si la gente compra pilas recargables, se tirarán menos pilas y por lo tanto la contaminación a causa de este residuo será menor.

Paso 2. Exchange this information with another pair. You will respond to the other pair's statements with a pessimistic view that presents a highly hypothetical situation.

MODELO: El reciclaje de pilas y el uso de pilas recargables
Bueno, si los grandes almacenes de electrónica tuvieran un contenedor para reciclar las pilas, la gente las guardaría y las llevaría a estos centros para reciclarlas, pero esto no va a ocurrir en un futuro próximo.

15-6 ¿Cómo sería mi vida si . . .? Imagine what your life would be like if you lived in a Spanish-speaking country, spoke Spanish, and your social life and environment were radically different. For instance, if you currently live in a small town, imagine living in a huge Latin American metropolis, working in a totally different job, having a completely different social life, etc.

Paso 1. Work with a partner to develop your hypothetical "other life." Make a list of your current life conditions and your "other life" conditions.

MI VIDA REAL	MI VIDA "HISPANA"

Paso 2. Write a short paragraph in which you present your thoughts on your "other life."
Start your paragraph with the phrase **Si yo fuera hispano/a . . .**

Si yo fuera hispano/a . . .

_____

_____

_____

_____

_____

_____

_____

_____

_____

_____

_____

_____

_____

_____

_____

_____

_____

_____

_____

_____

15-7 Cuentos imposibles. The following are the beginnings of impossible tales adapted from well-known stories.

- Si Superman no tuviera una capa . . .

- Si el lobo se comiera a Caperucita Roja . . .

- Si los Tres Cerditos construyeran sus casas de piedra . . .

- Si la Cenicienta no perdiera su zapato . . .

- Si Blancanieves no mordiera la manzana . . .

- Si el Príncipe no besara en los labios a la Bella Durmiente . . .

The class will be divided into groups. The teacher will give a transparency and a marker to each group, with one of the previous phrases on it.

Paso 1. First, with your group, finish the opening phrase of this unlikely tale. You will have one minute to complete it. Pass the transparency on to the group of students on your right, and receive the transparency from the group on your left. Continue the story by expressing another condition. Continue passing on the transparencies until all groups have contributed all the stories.

MODELO: Si Superman no tuviera una capa, . . .
          (GRUPO 1) → *no podría saltar desde los rascacielos.*
          (GRUPO 2) → *Si no pudiera saltar desde los rascacielos, no podría salvar a la personas.*
          (GRUPO 3) → *Si no pudiera salvar a las personas, etc.*

Paso 2. Once you receive your story back, you will write the final sentence. Then, share all the stories on the overhead projector with the whole class. Have fun!

3. *Se* for unplanned occurrences

15-8 Tu amigo patoso.

Student A: You left your apartment in the care of a friend. When you come back from your vacation, your apartment is in a chaotic state. You confront your friend with questions regarding this careless behavior.

Student B: You took care of your friend's apartment for a couple of weeks, but somehow your house-sitting experience did not go well. Your friend accuses you of wrongdoing. You will answer trying to avoid any responsibility for the unfortunate events.

Problemas:

La computadora no funciona.

No encuentras las llaves del coche.

Las plantas están muertas.

Las ventanas están abiertas.

La alfombra está mojada.

El correo no aparece por ninguna parte.

El gato ha desaparecido.

No hay línea telefónica en el apartamento.

. . .

Nombre: _____   **Fecha:** _____

MODELO: *La computadora no funciona. ¿La has usado?*
         ¡No, se te olvidó apagarla antes de marcharte!

E1: _____

E2: _____

E1: _____

E2: _____

E1: _____

E2: _____

E1: _____

E2: _____

E1: _____

E2: _____

E1: _____

E2: _____

E1: _____

E2: _____

E1: _____

E2: _____

E1: _____

E2: _____

MOSAICOS

15-9 Una historia fantástica. Read again *Apocalipsis I* by Marco Denevi on page 520 of the textbook. Following the tone of this story, create a short story in which an unlikely narrator (for instance, an alien) tells the story of the end of a current contribution to the progress of humankind; for example, the end of vehicle transportation, computers, current forms of energy, literate societies, modern medicine, etc. Be as creative as you can!

Paso 1. Work on the creation of the protagonist, the tone, and the temporal reference (time of the story) with a classmate.

- the situation

- the triggering of events

- the development of events

- the denouement of the story

- disclosure of the narrating voice

Other considerations:

- the tone of the story: funny? sad? dark?

- the tense of the narration: Is it a prediction? Is it a hypothesis? Has it already occurred?

Paso 2. Write your story, and read it to the whole class or a group of students. At the end, you will vote for the best story of all. Make sure to give it a title.

15-10 Crucigrama. Find eight words related to the environment in this crossword puzzle. Review page 525 of your textbook to complete this exercise.

1. Lo que ocurre cuando se cortan árboles pero no se replantan. _____

2. La _____ del Canal de Panamá es un enorme valle artificial por donde fluye una gran masa de agua.

3. El ambiente donde se desarrollan los seres vivos. _____

4. La recolección de los alimentos en ciertas temporadas del año. _____

5. La más famosa de América es la del Amazonas. _____

6. Debemos proteger los _____ naturales de las zonas en peligro.

7. El primer _____ hispanoamericano se llama Chang Díaz.

8. Los científicos se preguntan si hay _____ en otros planetas.

Nombre: _____   Fecha: _____

ENFOQUE CULTURAL

15-11 Un negocio de importación. As part of your international economics class, you ne
to create a business that imports Latin American products. You will research the different
food industries Spanish-speaking countries offer. You can find information at the website
http://www.guiadelmundo.com.

Sample markets:

industria vitivinícola (Chile, Argentina)

pescados y mariscos congelados (Chile, Perú)

frutas tropicales (Centroamérica)

flores (Colombia)

carnes (Argentina)

productos derivados del petróleo (Venezuela)

lanas y textiles (Guatemala, Uruguay)

café (Colombia, Costa Rica)

Paso 1. You will focus on two related markets only. List the products that can be marketed
the United States, the state of processing (raw, manufactured, etc.), the method of transport
intermediaries, market destinations.

Producto: *Producto:*

_____   _____

_____   _____

_____   _____

_____   _____

_____   _____

_____   _____

_____   _____

Paso 2. Present your import business plan to your classmates. Make sure you first describe the product and give information about the region. Then, present reasons why you have chosen this product and how you will market it, from the time of acquisition to its sale in U.S. markets. Additionally, you may be able to do some basic research on the market value of the products in their country of origin, and estimate the profit you may obtain by selling the products in the United States. Use visual aids to create a convincing presentation.

15-12 El cine latino. The film industries of Argentina, Colombia, Cuba, and Mexico have reached the audiences of the United States, and their film directors and stars have received international recognition in recent years. Do research on five recent movies (less than five years old) from any of these countries that are currently showing in local cinemas or are available at local video stores.

Paso 1. Bring a list to class and decide, as a whole class, which one you would like to see together. If possible, choose a movie that depicts issues related to progress, modern life, technology, and other topics discussed in *Capítulo 15*. Go to the movie theater as a group, or watch the movie in or out of class. Advertise it to other Spanish classes and have a great Spanish-speaking movie experience!

Paso 2. In class, discuss different aspects of the movie you viewed. Work with a classmate or a group of students, and share your answers with the whole class.

1. Escribe de cinco a diez palabras nuevas que has aprendido viendo esta película.

_____   _____

_____   _____

_____   _____

_____   _____

_____   _____

2. Nombra los personajes principales, y descríbelos físicamente y de acuerdo a su personalidad.

_____

_____

_____

_____

3. Escribe un breve resumen de la trama (*plot*).

_____

_____

_____

_____

4. ¿Cuáles son los temas de la película? Escribe una lista.

_____

_____

_____

5. Escribe un diálogo de una escena importante de la película con tu compañero/a.

Escena: _____

_____

_____

_____

_____

_____

_____

_____

_____

6. Ahora, representa la escena para un grupo de estudiantes o para toda la clase.

Apéndice

Nombre: _____

Fecha: _____

LECCIÓN PRELIMINAR

P-11. Las horas

Student B

PELÍCULA	SESIONES			
La mujer araña	12:30	3:20	6:10	9:45
La casa de los espíritus	12:15	2:30	4:45	8:40
Diarios de motocicleta	1:10	4:00	7:35	10:25
Hable con ella	-----	5:10	8:05	10:50
Troya	2:40	6:10	9:30	11:05

LECCIÓN 1

1-6. El plano de la universidad. Paso 2.

Student B

El plano de la universidad

Student B

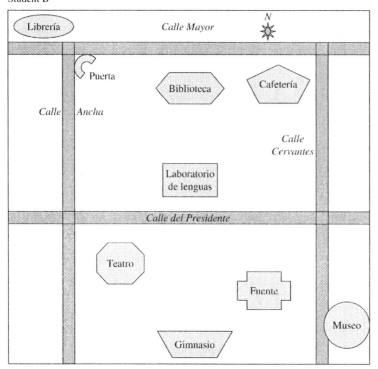